Pocket
HISTORY
of the
CHURCH

D. JEFFREY BINGHAM

InterVarsity Press
Downers Grove, Illinois

InterVarsity Press
P.O. Box 1400, Downers Grove, IL 60515-1426
World Wide Web: www.ivpress.com
E-mail: mail@ivpress.com

*InterVarsity Press® is the book-publishing division of InterVarsity Christian Fellowship/
USA®, a student movement active on campus at hundreds of universities, colleges and
schools of nursing in the United States of America, and a member movement of the
International Fellowship of Evangelical Students. For information about local and
regional activities, write Public Relations Dept., InterVarsity Christian Fellowship/USA,
6400 Schroeder Rd., P.O. Box 7895, Madison, WI 53707-7895, or visit the IVCF website
at <www.ivcf.org>.*

All Scripture quotations, unless otherwise indicated, are taken from the Holy Bible, New
International Version® . NIV®. *Copyright ©1973, 1978, 1984 by International Bible
Society. Used by permission of Zondervan Publishing House. All rights reserved.*

Cover photograph: Cologne, Germany/Superstock

ISBN 0-8308-2701-3

Printed in the United States of America ∞

Library of Congress Cataloging-in-Publication Data

Bingham, D. Jeffrey (Dwight Jeffrey)
  Pocket history of the church / D. Jeffrey Bingham.
     p. cm.
  Includes bibliographical references and indexes.
  ISBN 0-8308-2701-3 (pbk.: alk. paper)
   1. Church history. I. Title
 BR145.3 .B56 2002
 270—dc21

                                                              2001051995

P	14	13	12	11	10	9	8	7	6	5
Y	13	12	11	10	09	08	07			

For my father,
and in loving memory
of my mother
(August 6, 1927 – November 8, 2001)

Contents

Preface

Bill Cosby recounts the following conversation between himself and a boy named Arthur:

> "Tell me, Arthur, how would you change history?"
> "I would leave out that part that's taught in school," he replied.
> "Then I'm afraid that not much would have happened."
> "That's okay. Too much stuff happened anyway."[1]

Arthur expressed the key issue with which I struggled in writing this book. Too much stuff did happen. In order to deal with this problem I have had to be very selective in what I discussed. As a result, you will not find here a general or broad overview to the history of the church. Instead you will find selections from church history that I believe to be particularly important to evangelical Christianity in the twenty-first century. This is a church history meant to help frame Christian emphases in the present day. The choices, of course, involve personal viewpoints, but they are informed by several years of teaching church history to evangelicals in a seminary setting. I do not pretend that the selections will go unchallenged. My goal is to nurture Christian virtues—faith, hope and love—through historical perspective. By demonstrating Christian vitality and weakness in each age, I hope to bring sober reflection upon our own expressions of Christianity. By introducing some major paradigms and issues, I intend to provide a succinct summary that will energize further reading and study. I hope to convince the reader that history aids spirituality. For helpful, one-volume introductions to fill in the gaps of this book, you may want to read *Christianity Through the Centuries* by Earle Cairns, *Turning Points* by Mark Noll, *Church History in Plain Language* by Bruce Shelley, and *Exploring Church History* by Howard Vos.

Not everyone will agree with my selections, and some may be disappointed in a gap I did not fill. To those readers I apologize. And that reminds me of something Will Rogers said about history and historians: "History ain't what it is; it's what some writer wanted it to be."[2]

Every historian is an interpreter of historical facts, presenting those facts as he or she understands them. The historian attempts to find some meaning or significance in what has happened in the past and to describe a relationship between this person and another, between this event and that one. Historians try to make connections and, out of those connections, to suggest lessons. This book presents what I believe to be the *significance* of several events and persons, not just a collection of facts and dates. Christians need to be helped by history, not burdened with all that "stuff that happened." To this end, at times I indicate continuity that historical beliefs and practices had with Scripture. In many ways church history is the history of Christians interpreting the Bible. That interpretation shows itself in a variety of ways, from commentaries to liturgy and from the practice of discipleship to the production of conciliar creeds. Furthermore, occasionally I will mention ways in which contemporary Christian writers evidence commonality with their historical relatives. Significance is highlighted through continuity.

That brings me back to Bill Cosby. The comedian said,

"Another young scholar, a girl of seven, was equally enlightening when I discussed history with her. 'Do you happen to know what Labor Day is?' I asked her. 'Labor Day is the day when everything is on sale,' she said."[3] Yes, we are after the significance of dates, people and events—but not just any significance. We want to see the significance for Christian perspective in the new century.

So, what in history may be of particular use to Christians of the twenty-first century? Let me suggest three things.

First, history can help us put our own experience, knowledge and practice into proper perspective. Each generation is tempted to view itself as the best, brightest and most insightful generation. Each generation of Christians is tempted to see its way of worship, its way of ministry, its way of doing spirituality as the most biblical or practical. History reminds us that our generation is not the only one that has ever lived the Christian life. We are Christians within a company of Christians, both present and past, both living on earth and with the Lord. History helps keep us from becoming infatuated with ourselves. History nurtures the godly virtue of humility.

Second, history reminds us that actions and ideas have consequences not only in our own generation but also for generations to come. What we believe, teach and practice affects future generations of believers. Therefore history helps us to not act or teach impulsively. We must employ caution. We must enter into self-criticism and self-evaluation. History helps keep us from taking ourselves too seriously, as if we had all the best answers. At the same time history helps us take ourselves very seriously, because we affect others.

Third, history can give us new ideas, new ways of thinking, new examples of practice that may be biblical. Because these treasures of life and faith are old, because they have been locked away in that dusty old chest of history, when we finally open it up and take them out, they seem new. Wise Christians should always be historians in one sense. They sit higher and can see further, more panoramically, if they enrich themselves from the past. John of Salisbury (1115–1180), a medieval scholar, spoke of the jewels, the riches, the prestige of antiquity. He was right. The past has bequeathed to us its gems. Note his wise words:

> Our own generation enjoys the legacy bequeathed to it by that which preceded it. We frequently know more, not because we have moved ahead by our own natural ability, but because we are supported by the [mental] strength of others, and possess riches that we have inherited from our forefathers. Bernard of Chartres used to compare us to [puny] dwarfs perched on the shoulders of giants. He pointed out that we see more and farther than our predecessors, not because we have keener vision or greater height, but because we are lifted up and borne aloft on their gigantic stature.[4]

Our brothers and sisters from the past, indwelt by the same Spirit who indwells us, have left us a rich inheritance. It's locked away inside a treasure chest. It's layered in cobwebs. It's rusty and in some ways not very appealing. But inside is the wealth John of Salisbury told us about: diamonds, emeralds, gold sovereigns and chains of Spanish silver. If you have ever wanted to go on a treasure hunt, you've come to the right place. We've already found the chest. The hard, laborious work is done. All we need do is dip our hands inside and let the riches run through our fingers. Come along, and you'll be sitting higher and seeing further.

Acknowledgments

I recognize with appreciation the support of several friends and colleagues: Craig Blaising, Doug Blount, John Hannah, George Hanson, Glenn Kreider, John Lippert, Beth and Wayne Motley, David Puckett, Steve Spencer and Roy Zuck. I appreciate also the enriching labor of my editor, Gary Deddo, and his colleagues at InterVarsity Press.

I also want to thank Marti, my sister, who led me gently and truthfully into the grand Christian story.

And of course I owe an overwhelming debt of gratitude to my wife, Pamela. She encourages and endures, with grace and charity, the pursuits of a historian.

Part 1

Diamonds
The Early Church

There I was in the catacombs outside Rome. I was thrilled, curious and fully attentive to what the guide was saying. Never mind that in my haste to get inside I had accidentally joined a German group with a German-speaking guide. These sites of ancient Christian burial held my eye captive. I'm sure my mouth hung open. I stared. I got chilled although I was wearing a coat.

This was the second burial site I had visited in as many days. The day before, I had taken a train south to Anzio, Italy, to the American cemetery where the fallen brave of World War II were buried. I had visited the museum of the great amphibious landing of January 1944, and I had walked what I thought was the invasion beach. Gazing out to sea and then back to the city, I tried to envision the ships, the landing craft and the troops. Now here I was walking below ground at the very place where some of my earliest brothers and sisters in Christ rested, awaiting the resurrection of their bodies. After all, as our guide reminded us, their bodies, even in death, are the temples of the Holy Spirit. Their loved ones had left artwork and inscriptions symbolic of their faith. Here slept Christians who even in death had a living hope. Sharing with their Lord the scorn of death, for them too the tomb was merely temporary.

My favorite figure in this early Christian art is that of the Good Shepherd.[1] Jesus is shown as a young man wearing a short tunic that hangs over his left shoulder and down to his knees. On his back he carries a lamb with his hand or arms wrapped firmly around the front and back legs. The symbolism is obvious: the Savior mercifully and securely saves the soul that was lost (Lk 15:3-7; Jn 10:1-16).

In a fourth-century fresco the Shepherd stands in a garden, surrounded by sheep that are refreshed by luscious, green grasses and by two men who soothe their parched throats in clear, blue waterfalls. Here are souls, rescued by the Savior, in paradise. The lovely scene evokes in the viewer's mind the words of Isaiah 49:9-10:

> They will feed beside the roads
> and find pasture on every barren hill.
> They will neither hunger nor thirst. . . .
> He who has compassion on them will guide them
> and lead them beside springs of water.

Of all the early inscriptions, I find my heart drawn most to the one that marked the grave of Damasus, bishop of Rome (366–384):

> He who trod the tumultuous waves,
> He who restores life to the seeds
> which die in the earth,
> He who could unloosen the lethal bonds of death
> after darkness,

> and restore life after three days
> to Martha's brother,
> will, I believe, make Damasus rise from his ashes.[2]

Here was the faith of the early church. I left the catacombs humbled, taught and inspired. But in this underground cemetery next to the Appian Way I had only just scratched the surface of the riches of the early church. There was—and is—so much more.

In part one of this book we see what some elements of leadership and Christian life looked like in the church from the close of the New Testament through the fifth century. One of the themes that continually shows itself is that Christians of the early church had to be doctrinally minded; they had to be astute theologically. Some other themes, equally important, are

☐ the emphasis on the corporate unity of the church rather than on individualism;

☐ the seriousness of Jesus' call to self-denial;

☐ the need to engage the outside world in understanding the Christian faith; and

☐ the definition of the church, the body of Christ, and its distinguishing features.

1

On the Heels
of the Apostles

WITH THE DEATH OF THE APOSTLES, the early church faced with enhanced concern the questions of unity, authority, persecution and the measure of truth. The New Testament books had not yet been collected. Various interpretations of the apostles' teaching and the Old Testament were rampant and in some cases were seductive and dangerous. False teachers continued to threaten the faith of believers as they had done in the days of Paul, Peter and John (1 Tim 1:3-7; 2 Pet 2:1-3; 1 Jn 2:18-19, 26). Factious envy and pride within communities of Christians continued to divide the churches (compare 1 Cor 3:1-4). And the persecution of Christians so common in the earliest days of Christianity bled into the second century (Acts 8:1; 1 Cor 4:9-13; Gal 1:13; 2 Thess 1:4 and 2 Tim 3:12).

The Apostolic Fathers

Worship and discipleship as Christ's community in humble unity, doctrinal truth and self-denial—this theme held captive the pens of the earliest Christian writers outside the Bible. These Christians are known as the "apostolic fathers" to indicate their close connection to the times of the apostles. Though some of their documents evidence a lengthy process of composition, involving perhaps different authors and editors, the versions we may read today seem to be dated to between A.D. 90 and 174. They are small yet precious gems that glitter with the features of Christianity immediately after the New Testament, from the close of the first century to the latter part of the second. Of these writings, especially noteworthy are the following: (1) the letter of *1 Clement* (A.D. 96–98), written by the bishop of Rome to the Christians of Corinth; (2) the letters of Ignatius, bishop of Antioch (ca. A.D. 110), written to several churches, including the Ephesians, Romans, Magnesians and Philadelphians; and (3) the *Martyrdom of Polycarp,* an account of the death of Polycarp (A.D. 155), bishop of Smyrna, sent in the form of a letter from the church of Smyrna to the church of Philomelium of Phrygia in what is today southern Turkey.

One particular occurrence of the disruption of Christian peace and unity was the division of the Corinthian church at the end of the first century, some forty years after Paul had written 1 Corinthians. Apparently younger, insolent members of the church had challenged and deposed honored bishops (presbyters) within the community for illegitimate reasons. So it is no surprise that Clement, in his letter to the Christians in Corinth, exhorted them to embrace humility: "Let us therefore be humble, brothers, laying aside all arrogance and conceit and foolishness and anger, and let us do what is written. For the Holy Spirit says: 'Let not the wise man boast about his wisdom, nor the strong about his strength, nor the rich about his wealth; but let him who boast, boast in the Lord, that he may seek him out, and do justice and righteousness.' "[1]

Furthermore, Clement reminded his readers about the nature of the presbyter's or bishop's office (there was as yet no distinction between a presbyter and a bishop) and about its relationship to Christ and the apostles. For Clement, bishops were holders of a permanent office instituted by the apostles. The apostles had appointed the first bishops and they had intended the office to continue after their deaths. After the apostles, bishops were to be appointed by other reputable leaders with the church's consent. Such men were not to be removed unjustly. In Clement's letter the word *bishops* always occurs in the plural, so we assume that a plurality of bishops existed in both Rome and Corinth. Since the first ones had connections to the apostles, and since the apostles had connections to Christ, the bishop's office was viewed seriously. Humility was required of those in this office. In this light, addressing the arrogant ones, Clement commanded, "You, therefore, who laid the foundation of the revolt, must submit to the presbyters and accept discipline leading to repentance, bending the knees of your heart."[2]

Clement's particular interest was the Corinthian church's humility before their church leaders. But this was just one aspect of his larger concern for the great Christian virtue of submissiveness. It was this virtue, he said, that would lead to unity within the church.

Clement's epistle reminds us that one of the essential components of Christianity is humility. He provides an Old Testament theology of the virtue. In *1 Clement* 13 he cites Jeremiah 9:23-24:

> "Let not the wise man boast of his wisdom
>   or the strong man boast of his strength
>   or the rich man boast of his riches,
> but let him who boasts boast about this:
>   that he understands and knows me,
> that I am the LORD, who exercises kindness,
>   justice and righteousness on the earth,
>   for in these I delight," declares the LORD.

At the end of the same chapter Clement quotes Isaiah 66:2:

> This is the one I esteem:
>> he who is humble and contrite in spirit,
>> and trembles at my word.

And *1 Clement* 18 includes a quotation of Psalm 51:17:

> The sacrifices of God are a broken spirit;
>> a broken and contrite heart,
>> O God, you will not despise.

Clement's emphases run parallel with those of Peter and Paul: "Submit to one another out of reverence for Christ" (Eph 5:21). "Young men, in the same way be submissive to those who are older. All of you clothe yourselves with humility toward one another, because, 'God opposes the proud but gives grace to the humble'" (1 Pet 5:5). "The elders who direct the affairs of the church well are worthy of double honor, especially those who whose work is preaching and teaching" (1 Tim 5:17).

According to the letters of Ignatius, leadership played a critical role in establishing church unity and correct doctrine. However, his letters reflect a situation in which, instead of there being several bishops in a location, there was a single bishop. Ignatius wrote his letters while he was being taken to Rome to be martyred. Arrested in Antioch because of his leadership in an "illegal" religion (Christianity), Ignatius composed epistles that continued to influence the Christian communities of Asia Minor and Rome. He had these special concerns:

☐ the false doctrines that were entering these communities

☐ the temptation, because of persecution, for believers to blend Jewish traditions with their Christian faith or to depart to Judaism

☐ the need for unity among the believers in light of these two dangers

The one doctrinal aberration that seemed especially to capture Ignatius's attention pertained to the person of Christ.

Some false teachers were promoting Docetism, the belief that Christ only seemed or appeared to be human and to possess actual flesh. The apostle John had already encountered a similar denial of Christ's flesh in the communities to which he had written his first epistle. He had dealt with it seriously: "This is how you can recognize the Spirit of God," he told his readers as he warned them about false prophets. "Every Spirit that acknowledges that Jesus Christ has come in the flesh is from God, but every spirit that does not acknowledge Jesus [as having come in the flesh] is not from God. This is the spirit of the antichrist" (1 Jn 4:2-3). Earlier, at the very beginning of the same letter, John had emphasized the importance of Christ's real flesh. The apostles had "heard . . . seen . . . looked at . . . [and] touched . . . the Word of life" (Jesus), whom they preached (1:1). Christians emphasize the reality and fullness of Jesus Christ's physical human flesh as well as his full deity.

Taking the threat of Docetism just as seriously as John did, Ignatius emphasized both Christ's deity and Christ's humanity. "There is only one physician, who is both flesh and spirit, born and unborn, God in man, true life in death, both from Mary and from God, first subject to suffering and then beyond it, Jesus Christ our Lord" (*Ephesians* 7.2).[3]

Ignatius also spoke directly of Christ's humanity, as seen in his death and resurrection. Writing to the Smyrnaeans (1.2—3.1), Ignatius said that Jesus was "truly nailed in the flesh for us under Pontius Pilate and Herod the Tetrarch . . . and he truly suffered just as he truly raised himself—not as certain unbelievers say, that he suffered in appearance only. . . . For I know and believe that he was in the flesh even after the resurrection."[4]

In addition to being influenced by false teachers who were spreading heresies about Christ's person, the churches of Asia Minor were also being influenced by Judaizers. The apostle Paul had been concerned that some Christians were interested in returning to the traditions of Judaism (Gal 4:8-11). Ignatius, too, was concerned that Judaizers would lead believers to depart from grace and Christ. Like Paul, Ignatius believed that a return to the Jewish communal legislation would be a return to practices now superseded by Christ's incarnation, death and resurrection. Ignatius wrote, "Do not be deceived by strange doctrines or antiquated myths, since they are worthless. For if we continue to live in accordance with Judaism, we admit that we have not received grace.... How can we possibly live without him [Jesus], whom even the prophets, who were his disciples in the Spirit, were expecting as their teacher? . . . Therefore, having become his disciples, let us learn to live in accordance with Christianity.... It is utterly absurd to profess Jesus Christ and to practice Judaism" *(Magnesians* 8.1—10.3).[5]

Against these threats to the Christian community fostered by the Docetists and Judaizers, Ignatius emphasized the need for unity. For him, division within the community of believers resulted from a failure to maintain a belief in the unity of Christ's two natures, the unity of God and the unity of the church around the Lord's Table. He said that believing that Christ was both human and divine was basic to unity in Christian communities. The unity of these two natures in Jesus was a model for unity in the church. If one denied the unity of Christ, as the Docetists did, he or she could also deny the oneness of Christ's body.

Ignatius also believed that faith in the unity of God was another essential component of oneness in Christian community. This meant believing that the one true God was perfectly revealed in Jesus. It meant holding to the oneness between Jesus and the Father, between Jesus and the God of the Old Testament. Denial of the intimate relationship between Father and Son—a denial fostered by the Judaizers' attempt to return Christians to the legislation of the Old Testament and thereby to diminish the revelation of Jesus—ultimately led to division in the church. If the Father and Son are not one, then brothers and sisters in Christ have little basis for unity. In Ignatius's emphasis on the connection between the unity of Father and Son and the church's unity one can almost hear an echo of the Lord's prayer in John 17:20-23:

> My prayer is not for them [the apostles] alone. I pray also for those who will believe in me through their message, that all of them may be one, Father, just as you are in me and I am in you. May they also be in us so that the world may believe that you have sent me. I have given them the glory that you gave me, that they may be one as we are one: I in them and you in me. May they be brought to complete unity to let the world know that you sent me and have loved them even as you have loved me.

In Ignatius's emphasis on the importance of a common faith we can also sense Paul's words. Paul reminded the Ephesian church of the "one faith" (Eph 4:5) and taught them that the purpose of the diverse gifts of apostles, prophets, evangelists, pastors and teachers (or pastor-teachers) was to build the church up "until we all reach unity in the faith and in the knowledge of the Son of God" (4:13).

To this same end (unity in faith) Ignatius pleaded for the unity of believers around submission to the bishop. But where Clement of Rome had defended the authority of a plurality of bishops on the grounds of apostolic succession, Ignatius viewed the authority of the single bishop on other grounds. For him the authority of the bishop was modeled after the authority of God the Father, "the Bishop of all" *(Magnesians* 3.1).[6] Believers, he said, are to show their devotion to God by their submission to the bishop *(Magnesians* 5). Since a bishop is a representative of truth, godliness is shown through submission to the bishop and through a common belief with other Christians. Ignatius wrote to Polycarp, bishop of Smyrna, "Focus on unity, for there is nothing better" (1.2).[7] Similarly, to the Ephesians he said, "There is nothing better than peace" (13.2).[8] Also

he urged the Philadelphians, "Do nothing without the bishop
. . . love unity. Flee from divisions. Become imitators of Jesus
Christ, just as he is of his Father" (7.2).[9] And to the Magnesians
he wrote, "Do not attempt to convince yourselves that anything
done apart from the others is right, but gathering together, let
there be one prayer, one petition, one mind, one hope, with
love and blameless joy, which is Jesus Christ, than whom nothing is better" (7.1).[10]

Some Protestants tend to see in Ignatius's writings an
emphasis on a domineering bishop, which later led to certain
abuses by the Roman papacy in the Middle Ages. In Clement's
and Ignatius's writing we see steppingstones that led to an
emphasis later on the Roman bishop and eventually the papacy.
But Ignatius's interest was the unity of the believing community
in the apostles' doctrine. The bishop was the truth's guardian,
for he knew the true meaning of Jesus' life, death, burial, resurrection, appearances, ascension and eventual return. He stood
in contrast to the Docetists and Judaizers, who were seducing
young Christians by means of doctrinal error. Ignatius's heartbeat was a concern that believers be united in common submission to apostolic doctrine. When they agreed with the bishop,
they agreed with the apostles and with God.

Furthermore, formal agreement with the apostle's teaching
took place not privately in isolation from the community but
rather occurred when the individuals came together in one
place for the Lord's Supper. The meal signified the church's
center around the actual fleshly, bloody death of Christ, a center that opposed the false teaching of both Docetists and
Judaizers. Sharing the Lord's Supper (the Eucharist) demonstrated the church's unity under the bishop: "Take care, therefore, to participate in one Eucharist (for there is one flesh of
our Lord Jesus Christ, and one cup which leads to unity
through his blood; there is one altar, just as there is one bishop,
together with the presbytery and the deacons, my fellow ser-

vants), in order that whatever you do, you do in accordance with God" *(Philadelphians* 4).

Ignatius's emphasis on Christian unity based on the apostles' doctrine and the Lord's Supper parallels the New Testament. The early Jerusalem church "devoted themselves to the apostles' teaching and to fellowship, to the breaking of bread and to prayer" (Acts 2:42). Paul had no praise for the Corinthians' selfish, divisive conduct when they came together for the Lord's Supper (1 Cor 11:17-34), conduct that made one "guilty of sinning against the body and blood of the Lord" (v. 27). Many were failing to wait for all believers to gather together before they ate. Thus they failed to honor the meaning of the *common* meal and were experiencing judgments including sickness and death. Paul pleaded with the Philippians to "make my joy complete by being like-minded, having the same love, being one in spirit and purpose. Do nothing out of selfish ambition or vain conceit, but in humility consider others better than yourselves" (Phil 2:2-3). And to Titus, the apostle wrote, "Warn a divisive person once, and then warn him a second time. After that, have nothing to do with him. You may be sure that such a man is warped and sinful; he is self-condemned" (Tit 3:10-11).

In addition to the concerns for unity and truth in community shared by Clement and Ignatius, the apostolic fathers shared an additional feature: persecution and martyrdom. We have already noted that Ignatius penned his letters as he was on the road to martyrdom. We pause now to consider his perspective on that impending eventuality and to, with awe, observe a record of the martyrdom of one faithful Christian, the bishop Polycarp.

For Ignatius, as for many early Christians, martyrdom was discipleship. When modern eyes read his statement about his favorable anticipation of death at Roman hands, a common response is to suggest that he had a serious neurotic dysfunction. But this response fails to understand how the second-century church viewed itself in relation to Jesus' death. We must try to understand the early Christians. After the Lord had predicted his own shame and suffering, he taught the crowds and disciples that Christianity involved imitating him:

> If anyone would *come after* me, he must *deny* himself and take up his *cross* and *follow* me. For whoever wants to save his life will *lose* it, but whoever *loses his life* for me and for the gospel will save it. What good is it for a man to gain the whole world, yet forfeit his soul? Or what can a man give in exchange for his soul? If anyone is *ashamed* of me and my words in this adulterous and sinful generation, the Son of Man will be *ashamed* of him when he comes in his Father's glory with the holy angels. (Mk 8:34-38, italics added)

For the second-century believer, since discipleship meant following Christ, then being his disciple may very well involve stepping into the blood-soaked footprints left by Jesus under the cross. To rebel against martyrdom—that is, to retreat—would be a failure to imitate Jesus in his quiet submission to death (Is 53:7; Mt 27:14; Mk 15:5; Lk 23:9; Jn 19:9). Cowardice would mean a believer was disobedient to the words Peter penned years after his own shameful failure in discipleship: "To this *you were called,* because Christ suffered for you, *leaving you an example, that you should follow in his steps.* 'He committed no sin, and no deceit was found in his mouth' [Is 53:9]. When they hurled their insults at him, *he did not retaliate;* when he suffered, *he made no threats.* Instead, *he entrusted himself* to him who judges justly" (1 Pet 2:21-23, italics added).

Self-pity in the face of martyrdom would be a failure to imitate Jesus in his words to the women who mourned for him on his way to be crucified: "Daughters of Jerusalem," Jesus said, "do not weep for me; weep for yourselves and for your children" (Lk 23:28).

Ignatius's arrest and sure death were God's call to his next

footstep in Christlike discipleship. If the just Father had so
willed that he would die as his Lord had done, not asking for
release and not arguing his defense, then he was willing to die.
For this reason Ignatius wrote in his letter to the Romans, "I am
writing to all the churches and am insisting to everyone that I
die for God of my own free will—unless you hinder me. I
implore you: do not be 'unseasonably kind' to me. Let me be
food for the wild beast. . . . Then I will truly be a disciple of Jesus
Christ, when the world will no longer see my body" (4.1-2).[11]

Such accounts leave us stunned, perplexed and almost
incredulous. How, we demand, could a Christian be a masoch-
ist? How could a mature believer, a bishop, a church leader
hold such a bizarre view of death? In our culture—even our
Christian culture, which underscores self-fulfillment and self-
preservation—such statements appear grotesque, even repul-
sive. This view, however, may say more about the oddity of
modern Christianity and its view of what constitutes discipleship than about the eccentricity of Ignatius. He would not
embrace self-preservation at the expense of not imitating
Christ. He was willing to surrender to the Father's will because
he was not greater than his Master.

Though we have records of Ignatius's perspective on his
own martyrdom, we lack an account of his actual death. But we
do have the martyrdom account of the apostolic father Polycarp, bishop of Smyrna (ca. 155/156?). The account, written by
the church at Smyrna to the church at Philomelium (and other
Christian communities) honored Polycarp as one who was
noble, patient in endurance and loyal to the Master *(Martyrdom
of Polycarp* 1.2). He was passive and compliant in his arrest, even
setting a table of refreshment for the arresting officials. He
prayed two hours for all those he knew personally and for the
church spread throughout the world before he was taken to the
stadium. Brought before the proconsul, who attempted to per-
suade him to recant his Christianity, Polycarp replied, "For

eighty-six years I have been a servant, and he has done me no wrong. How can I blaspheme my King who saved me?"[12] So the proconsul said, "I have wild beasts; I will throw you to them, unless you change your mind." But Polycarp said, "Call for them! For the repentance from better to worse is a change impossible for us; but it is a noble thing to change from that which is evil to righteousness." Then the proconsul announced, "I will have you consumed by fire, since you despise the wild beasts, unless you change your mind." But Polycarp replied, "You threaten with a fire that burns only briefly and after just a little while is extinguished, for you are ignorant of the fire of the coming judgment and eternal punishment, which is reserved for the ungodly. But why do you delay? Come, do what you wish."[13]

From the beginning of the third century, and also from around the middle of the fourth century, we have other stunning accounts of Christian martyrdom. One records the faithfulness of a young mother, Perpetua, who was arrested along with five friends and martyred in 203.[14] Although she had an infant son and her pagan father tried desperately to convince her to deny that she was a Christian, she remained firm in her conviction. She insisted that she admit to being what she was— a Christian. Another account is one of several texts recording the martyrdom of Persian Christians. It tells us of the trial and execution of Martha, who followed her father, Posi, in martyrdom and who in the last words of her final prayer petitioned God to preserve the faith of the believers in her community and to strengthen them in a true trinitarian worship and confession.[15] Here again is the remarkable perspective on discipleship by the early church.

The Apologists

As the second century progressed, Roman criticism of Christianity continued to grow. However, this criticism was not unique to the apostolic fathers and the apologists. Already in the first century Suetonius, a Roman historian, had recorded that in Nero's reign Christians had been punished because they held to a novel, superstitious religion (*Lives of Caesars* 16.2). The Romans said the religions of many people were superstitious, including the Christians, the Egyptians and the Jews.[16] The Romans' polytheistic religion was central to their way of life, and all social events were religious in nature. If a religion (like Christianity) did not join hand in hand with Roman pagan society, it was often doomed to persecution. This happened because the Romans feared the punishment of their gods. If the Christians were allowed to disrupt the unity of Roman religion and society, the gods (the Romans believed) would bring curses on Rome.

Roman religion also was intimately related to the past. Greco-Roman society held that the rites of the ancients were more harmonious with the gods than the newer rites. That is, the past was closer to the ancient gods. For Roman society, only one ancient religious doctrine existed, and it was expressed and maintained in a variety of traditional forms by various nations. Abandonment of these variant but traditional forms and customs was wicked. Novelty in religions, they thought, was irreligious. Therefore, because Christians were seen as antisocial and "new," they were viewed as a danger to Rome. The gods were unhappy and had to be pacified.

When Christians worshiped only one God, their polytheistic Roman neighbors viewed them as atheistic. When Christians gathered in worship, separate from Roman life, they were seen as destructive to the social structure of the empire. In their refusal to confess the emperor's deity they were viewed as wicked. This refusal to engage in civic religion led the Christian apologist Tertullian to write that the Romans considered Christians "public enemies" and "enemies of Rome."[17]

But the Romans did not end their criticism of Christianity

with reference to what they viewed as irreligious. They also criticized Christianity for being irrational. Christians seemed to receive their teachings by faith rather than by rational examination of the evidence or critical thinking. According to the Christian theologian Origen, one Roman, Celsus, wrote that some Christians said, "Do not ask questions, only believe."[18]

Also, the Romans interpreted some Christian practices as deplorable because of what seemed to be a secretiveness, a ridiculous perspective of life, death and future judgment, an arrogant haughtiness toward Roman religion and a lifestyle of perversity. Minucius Felix, a Latin Christian apologist of the third century, recorded some early Roman understandings of Christian rites and beliefs. Many unbelievers thought that Christians were "a people skulking and shunning the light, silent in public but garrulous in corners. They despise the temples as dead-houses, they reject the gods, they laugh at sacred things. . . . They know one another by secret marks and insignia, and they love one another almost before they know one another. Everywhere also there is mingled among them a certain religion of lust, and they call one another promiscuously brothers and sisters."[19]

The belief that Christians were clandestine in their gatherings because of their shameful "incest" (because they married those they called "brother" and "sister") was common, as was the charge that they were cannibalistic (they ate the body of Christ and drank his blood). Because of the secret nature of their rites, and also because some groups claiming association with Christianity were reported to have engaged in acts of perversity, the rumors grew to absurd proportions. Christians were even accused of eating infants. The Christian apologist Athenagoras was accurate when he said, "Three charges are brought against us: atheism, Thyestean feasts [cannibalistic banquets] and Oedipean intercourse [incestuous unions]."[20]

As strange as it may sound to modern Christian ears, the

Romans were appalled at the supposed wickedness, social rebellion, irrationality and impiety of the Christians. The "popular and uncritical rumor" about Christians, to use the language of Athenagoras, set the tone for how the Romans responded. Of course, we ought not think that early Christianity was perfect or without blame. Many Christians did not balance their faith in the one true God through Jesus Christ with a biblical call to morality and state loyalty. In addition, some non-Christians who associated with believers were said to have practiced their Roman religion in feasts that *did* involve promiscuous rites.[21] On the whole, though, the charges of rampant perversity in Christ's body within the Roman Empire were false.

The apologists of the second century took it on themselves to defend the church against such charges. And though their work was done honorably, we should never forget that such accusations against the church motivated by hatred for Christ are not to be seen as strange or odd. Rather, they are to be taken as blessings, after the words of our Lord: "Blessed are you when people insult you, persecute you and falsely say all kinds of evil against you because of me. Rejoice and be glad, because great is your reward in heaven, for in the same way they persecuted the prophets who were before you" (Mt 5:11-12; see also Lk 6:22). What the second-century believers endured was fully in line with Jesus' promise. Erroneous views about Christianity that led to believers being marginalized socially, and incarcerated, tortured and killed, was consistent with what Jesus had said they could expect. Persecution is a blessing with reward (Jas 1:5, 12). As R. T. France, meditating on Jesus' promise of recompense for suffering, reminds us, "no-one will be a loser in any ultimate sense, by becoming a disciple of Christ."[22]

In their defense of Christianity before the Roman emperors the second-century apologists did not try to argue that suffering was harmful to the growth of Christianity. In fact they pointed out the opposite. Justin Martyr, a major apologist writing around 150-160, insisted that as Christians were tortured they did not renounce their confession in Christ (*Dialog with [the Jew] Trypho* 110-14). Instead large numbers of people were converted to Christianity because believers did not renounce their faith in the face of suffering. The *Letter to Diognetus*, an anonymous Christian apology of the second century, also stated that "Christians, when punished day by day increase more and more. It is to no less a post than this that God has ordered them, and they must not try and evade it."[23]

Neither did the apologists seek to justify any wickedness present in Christianity. Instead, they sought to explain what Christians really believed and what they really practiced. Persecution was the result, they believed, of uninvestigated charges, unreasonable emotions and demonic persecution (Justin, *First Apology* 5). They appealed for justice against slander, hopeful that an explanation of Christianity as reasonable, thoughtful, moral, civic-minded and ancient would result in toleration of their religion. Such appeals were made to the emperor's own sense of justice.

Two apologists, Justin Martyr and Athenagoras, are noted for the way they stood in the gap to defend Christianity. Of concern to both of them was that Christian morality be portrayed. In his *First Apology* (ca. 150) Justin described the lives of Christians this way:

> Those who once rejoiced in fornication now delight in continence alone; those who made use of magic arts have dedicated themselves to the good and unbegotten God; we who once took most pleasure in the means of increasing our wealth and property now bring what we have into common fund and share with everybody in need; we who hated and killed one another and would not associate with men of different tribes because of [their different] customs, now after the manifestation of Christ live together and pray for our enemies.[24]

Athenagoras wrote similarly in his *Plea for Christians* (ca. 177), as he contrasted Christian conduct with the conduct of those who were accepted and even honored by Rome: "When struck, they do not strike back; when robbed, they do not sue; to those who ask, they give; and they love their neighbors as themselves. If we did not think that a God ruled over the human race, would we live in such purity? The idea is impossible. But since we are persuaded that we must give an account of all our life here to God who made us and the world, we adopt a temperate, generous, and despised way of life."[25] Athenagoras also wrote, "We, however, cannot refrain from turning the cheek when we are struck, nor from blessing when we are reviled. For it is not enough to be just—justice consisting in returning blows—but we have to be generous and to put up with evil."[26] These challenging writings echo Jesus' words in the Sermon on the Mount in Matthew 5:38-48.

This second-century apologetic anticipated a small book written by Francis Schaeffer. In *The Mark of the Christian* he wrote on the basis of John 17:21 that the "final apologetic" was the love of Christians for each other. (John 17:21 records that Jesus prayed that the church may be in unity so that the world would believe that he is from the Father.) Schaeffer said, "We cannot expect the world to believe that the Father sent the Son, that Jesus' claims are true, and that Christianity is true, unless the world sees some reality of the oneness of true Christians."[27] The Christian ethic is always the first line of defense, whether in the second century or the twenty-first.

Justin and Athenagoras also informed the emperors about their civic loyalties, which they understood in good Roman fashion to be a constituent part of Christianity as well as Roman religion. For the apologists, being obedient to Christ and Paul's teachings included civic loyalty. Listen to Justin's words, written in times of persecution:

More even than others we try to pay the taxes and assessments to those whom you appoint, as we have been taught by him [Christ]. For once in his time some came to him and asked whether it were right to pay taxes to Caesar. And he answered, "Tell me, whose image is on the coin." They said, "Caesar's." And he answered them again, "Then give what is Caesar's to Caesar and what is God's to God" [Mt 22:20-21; Mk 2:14-17; Lk 20:22-25]. So we worship God only, but in other matters we gladly serve you.[28]

In addition to explaining Christian ethics and civic-mindedness, the apologists were also concerned with defending their monotheism against the charge of atheism. Athenagoras went to great length in arguing the reasonableness and the propriety of faith in only one God. He did so by appealing to the universe's order, to pagan poets and philosophers who were also monotheists, and to the rational argument that points up the implausibility of the existence of two or more sovereign, competing deities. Ultimately, however, he confessed that belief in the one true God on these bases would be merely human. The monotheistic faith of Christians is confirmed not by rational argumentation but by the ancient testimonies of the Spirit-inspired prophets, whom he cited (Ex 20:2-20; Is 43:10-11; 44:6; 66:1).[29]

In their effort to dispel charges of Christianity's offensive peculiarity, these second-century apologists helped build bridges between Christian thought and practice and the culture of Rome. In many ways their method was one of asking for toleration by demonstrating how similar they were to the tolerated mainstream or even to Rome's highest values. In a time when guilt by association with the name "Christian," fueled by paranoia and false understandings, led to persecution, such bridges were wise, could soothe fiery tempers and could give opportunity for further dialogue. The apologists knew the philosophy of the day and exploited it in communicating the reasonableness and acceptability of Christianity within their culture. But as has been shown, their faith and practice did not constitute a surrender to that culture but rather were a submission to the teachings of the prophets, the Lord and his disciples. In obeying the Scriptures they were saying, "We're not bad citizens. Nor are we bad Romans. Therefore don't believe the prejudiced crowds and persecute us. We're different but tolerable."

For the apologists the central Christian task had become one of explaining what Christianity actually was in the face of persecution. This is always a Christian task.

Irenaeus and the Heretics

The paranoia, hatred and misunderstanding of the Romans were not the only threats facing the church. The problem of Roman persecution came from *outside* the community, but the problem of heresy arose from *within* the church, from those who falsely claimed to be Christians. Though several groups of unorthodox people could be discussed, we will focus on two, the Gnostics and the Marcionites, and on one great churchman, Irenaeus of Lyon, who labored diligently to protect the church from their harmful teachings.

Around 180, Irenaeus wrote five books against the heresies that were threatening his people. The most prevalent heresy was Gnosticism. The Gnostics taught that salvation was based on a secret knowledge to which only they were privy. These false teachers were seducing members of Irenaeus's parish.

Come back with me to a marketplace in the center of the ancient city of Lugdunum, Gaul (now called Lyon, France). You and your spouse are shopping for fresh vegetables, the fish catch of the day and some oil for your household lamps. As you pause before the tomatoes and carrots displayed by the merchant Cletus, his nephew Marcus, a confessing Christian not part of Irenaeus's congregation, engages you in conversation. "So, I understand that you two regard yourselves as believers in Christ," he says with a smile.

"Yes," you respond. "We follow the teachings of our bishop, Irenaeus."

"Oh," he says sharply. "I'm a believer in Christ, who came to us in Jesus from the Father in order to reveal the truth about God to us. Is this what your community believes?"

"Yes, of course," you insist. "We're Christians."

"Well, I am not sure that Irenaeus has told you everything that's involved in truly being Christian."

You look at him curiously and ask, "What do you mean, 'not everything'? We believe exactly what you said you believe!"

"Oh, really," he replies with a smirk. "Let's go somewhere where we can talk—shall we?—and let me explain exactly what I believe and what your 'trustworthy' bishop Irenaeus is keeping from you. He wants to control you and prevent you from having what he can't have."

You follow Marcus through a dark doorway behind the vegetable stand where he begins to explain his "Christian" faith. When he finishes, you and your spouse are stunned. You look at each other open-mouthed. He had used the Old Testament and the writings of the Evangelists and Paul. He had spoken with such conviction and sincerity. He had used all the phrases, catchwords and Bible verses that you hear at your Lord's Supper and Scripture reading services. But although he sounded just like you, he hadn't meant the same thing. You and your spouse, having been under Irenaeus's teaching for several years, quickly thank Marcus and leave without another word. The newly baptized couple from your congregation who arrive at the vegetable stand as you leave, however, will not be as fortunate. Following is what Marcus the Gnostic had explained to you. It is one version of various forms of the Gnostic myth.

The "Father" whom Marcus had spoken of was the eternal, unknowable, spiritual, supreme deity. This Father had issued forth from himself spiritual beings known as Aeons. They had names like "Christ," "Logos," "Savior" and "Sophia." At some point "Sophia" decided inappropriately, with pride and arrogance, that she could and would arrive at a knowledge of the unknowable, highest Father. Her pride and arrogance resulted in her begetting another being named Yaldabaoth, who was known as the Demiurge, or Creator. He inherited his mother's faults of sin, pride, arrogance and evil. It was this being, not the highest Father, who created the physical world. For Marcus, then, the Creator—the God of the Old Testament, Yahweh of Israel—is *not* the supreme Father. He is an evil, arrogant, lower being. When he explained a prophetic passage such as Isaiah 46:9, in which God announced his exclusivity by saying, "I am God and there is no other," Marcus said this was the Demiurge pridefully asserting his uniqueness out of ignorance of the true Father. As a consequence the material world created by the Demiurge has the characteristics of the Creator. Everything physical, the earth and particularly the human body, is seen as evil, bad, even putrid.

Marcus then explained that there was an attempt by the good spiritual beings to correct the perversion of the creation of a physical world. But Yaldabaoth was able to capture some of the heavenly, spiritual elements and hold them captive within some *bad* physical bodies. Marcus called these spiritual elements "seeds of light," "the inner person," or most often, "the spirits." "So," Marcus had summarized, *"some* human bodies, putrid as they are, house the only valuable eternal element we call the spirit. There are two kinds of humans: those who have the seed or spirit (the elect) and those who don't. The ultimate goal, what I regard as *salvation,* is the release of the *real me,* my *spirit,* from my worthless body so that I can ascend back to the spiritual world. Ultimate salvation is my spirit flying away from this shell, this tomb, of the body."

"I suppose you are interested in how one can be saved," he asked slyly. Both of you had nodded yes, with eyes big as saucers. "Well, I believe that the spiritual being 'Christ' came from the Father to redeem the spirits imprisoned by the wicked Creator. He did this by revealing the true knowledge of the Father to us. Now, this 'Christ' being could not, of course, become a human, because that would entail having a putrid body. So either he merely appeared to be human or he simply indwelt a human named 'Jesus' by adopting him as his 'carrier,' his vehicle. So, you see, there are really two and not one. There is the human being, 'Jesus' (or merely the appearance of a human) and the spiritual being, 'Christ.' This Christ revealed to his disciples the *knowledge* that the Creator of the Old Testament is *not* the true God. The true God is the Father of Christ. It is this knowledge that saves and that releases my spirit from my body."

Such Gnostic theology was quite prominent in the second century and was a serious threat to the church. It employed the language of Christianity and even misused the Scriptures of Christianity to develop its system of belief. In essence it was *dualistic.* That is, it assigned extreme, opposite values to differing realities and utterly distinguished things that the Bible holds together: Spirit is good, but the body and other physical things are bad; the spiritual Father is the true, good God, but the Creator is a bad impostor; the spirit Christ is the true Savior, but the human Jesus is only a shell; elect humans are good, but other humans are dispensable; the New Testament is the good news of salvation, but the Old Testament is a record of false religion.

One tricky thing about Gnostics, Irenaeus thought, was that before they explained their system they *sounded* so orthodox, so biblical. Referring to Jesus' warning about false prophets in Matthew 7:15, Irenaeus frequently thought of them as "wolves in sheep's clothing." He wrote, "Such men are to outward appearance sheep; for they appear to be like us by what they say in public, repeating the same words as we do; but inwardly they are wolves."[30] He described them as those who have mixed up a poison and passed it off as a refreshing drink.[31]

The other tricky thing about Gnostics, for Irenaeus, was that they used the Scriptures to support their system. But *using* the Scripture, he pointed out, meant nothing. Anyone can use the Bible to support his or her position. Anyone can manipulate the Scriptures in an attempt to make them fit his or her views. All you need to do is pay attention to some parts, ignore other parts, take a sentence or a word here, connect that to a sentence or word there, and you have rewritten Scripture into a pattern that fits what you want it to say.

Irenaeus opposed the Gnostics by explaining to his Christian community the proper "fit" of Scripture in light of the traditional teachings of the church passed down from the apostles to the bishops. Irenaeus taught his congregation what the church had taught before the Gnostics showed up. He appreciated the strength that resulted from a healthy union between Scripture and tradition. The interpretation of Scripture passed down by the apostles and preserved by the bishops was a safeguard in the face of heretics who also appealed to Scripture. The issue brought to the foreground by the Gnostics was that anybody can appeal to Scripture. Anybody can "use" the Bible, but the question is, how are they interpreting the Bible?

Against the dualistic theology of the Gnostics, Irenaeus emphasized several doctrines. First, there exists only one God, who is both the Creator, the God of the Old Testament, and the Father of Jesus Christ. Second, Jesus is the incarnate, eternal Son and Word of the Father. Third, although there is some difference between the Old and New Testaments (before and after the incarnation), they are both parts of the one history of redemption. Fourth, since the Father, through his Son, is the Creator of the physical body and of the earth, the physical world has value. The body will be raised incorruptible and reunited with the immaterial part of the human (spirit, soul), and the earth, purified by fire, will be refashioned or renewed. Fifth, there is only one humanity, all of which is fallen and in need of redemption. There is no elitism in humanity, such as a distinction between the "spiritual ones" of the Father and the "material ones" of the Creator. Redemption is accomplished by the eternal Son of God, who became human and thereby through his incarnation united God with humanity. Jesus Christ as God *who is human* introduces into humanity's sad, decaying history a hope for humanity's immortality. As "the last Adam," Christ began a new line of humanity destined for eternal glory, and he reversed the cause and effect of the first Adam.

Most pointedly, what distinguished Irenaeus from the heretics was his theme of unity and his commitment to interpreting Scripture within the parameters of the faith passed down from apostle to bishop. What has been entrusted from one faithful Christian to another always plays an important role in interpretation.

To Irenaeus, tradition was an important source of information on what the Bible taught. It's not strange that we find the Bible itself speaking about the importance of heeding those faithful ones who have gone before us and passing on to others what we receive. Four times Paul wrote about this to Timothy:

> Timothy, guard what has been entrusted to your care. Turn away from godless chatter and the opposing ideas of what is falsely called knowledge, which some have professed and in so doing have wandered from the faith. (1 Tim 6:20-21)

> What you heard from me, keep as the pattern of sound teaching, with faith and love in Christ Jesus. Guard the good deposit that was entrusted to you—guard it with the help of the Holy Spirit who lives in us. (2 Tim 1:13-14)

> The things you have heard me say in the presence of many witnesses entrust to reliable men who will also be qualified to teach others. (2 Tim 2:2)

> Continue in what you have learned and have become con-
> vinced of, because you know those from whom you learned it.
> (2 Tim 3:14)

As we saw in Gnosticism, some people exploit Scripture for
their own ends. Therefore, what faithful Christians through
the years have been saying Scripture means can be helpful in
preventing our own misinterpretations. In Irenaeus's day the
central function of church leaders was to explain what the
prophets, the Lord and the apostles had meant by what they
had said. What Scripture said was given a formal interpretation,
which set the apostolic teaching apart from that of the heretics.
Anybody, it had become clear, could *say* they believed in Jesus
Christ as their personal Savior sent by the Father. But what did
they *mean* by terms like "Jesus Christ," "personal Savior" and
"Father"? Church leaders like Irenaeus explained the ways
those words and phrases were to be understood properly. I like
what Martin Marty says about Gnosticism: "Fusing a pagan
ancestry with Christian deviations, it knew many of the words
but little of the music of the song of Christian redemption."[32]

Another heresy that threatened the second century church
was Marcionism. Named after its founder, Marcion, it too held
that there are two Gods: a wrathful, judgmental one of the Old
Testament and a gracious, good one of the New. Marcion
viewed the Jews, their Scriptures and their religion as of no value because of their association with the "old God." His Bible,
therefore, included only New Testament books that in his judgment were antithetical to the "Law-oriented" religion of the
Jews. These books included only Luke's Gospel and ten of
Paul's Epistles. Irenaeus opposed Marcion in his *Against Heresies,* as did Tertullian in his *Against Marcion.* Again, these theologians emphasized the unity between the Testaments, which
reveals the unity of the one God and Father of both Israel and
the church.

Although Marcion answered the question incorrectly, the

question he asked is a pivotal one in Christian thinking: What is the relationship of the Old Testament, the law, and the religious faith and practice of Israel to the church? Marcion's answer was that there is no relationship.

Christians today still debate the relationship of the Old Testament law to believers. The Old Testament still struggles in many pulpits for equal time with the New. Certain pocket editions of the Bible can give believers the impression that only two Old Testament books—Psalms and Proverbs—are critical to their growth in Christ. The church as a whole has not reached a consensus on how to view the relationship between the two Testaments. However, early on the church dispensed quickly and firmly with Marcion's answer. Under the New Covenant, the church has an intimate connection to the history of salvation in the Old Covenant. The Old Testament anticipates the New; the New Testament fulfills, interprets and complements the Old. When Paul wrote "All Scripture is profitable" (2 Tim 3:16 KJV), he was thinking mainly of the Old Testament.

Heresy did not go away as the church matured. In the fourth and fifth centuries it would struggle with delineating properly the doctrines of the Trinity and Christ's person. Thankfully, gifted theologians would guide the church into the safety of the one true faith. This story awaits us in the next chapter.

2

Councils of Doctrine, Cloisters of Holiness

Iɴ ᴛʜᴇ ᴇᴀʀʟʏ ᴘᴀʀᴛ ᴏꜰ ᴛʜᴇ ꜰᴏᴜʀᴛʜ ᴄᴇɴᴛᴜʀʏ Christianity began to experience a new relationship with emperor and state. In A.D. 312 Constantine, emperor of Gaul and Britain, expanded his rule throughout the West by a decisive victory against his rival Maxentius. Following a vision, he pledged loyalty to Christianity, went into battle under Christian symbols, defeated Maxentius and credited his victory to the Christian God. This led to the empire's first pro-Christian policy, evidenced in the state's recognition of the Christian God and the easing of persecution. In 313 an agreement reached between Constantine and the co-emperor Licinius resulted in the Edict of Milan, which introduced a policy for the toleration of Christianity. Not until 380, however, did the emperor Theodosius I ban paganism and give Christianity the status of the state religion.

Although the threat of persecution was waning, heresy in the fourth century continued to be a critical concern. In the second century, in the face of the Gnostics and the Marcionites, the church had to press for belief in the unity of the Old and New Testaments. But the church in the fourth century faced the critical concern of the unity between God the Father and his Son. The trinitarian controversy—which struggled with how Christians were to describe the relationship between the Father and the Son and, later, the Spirit—began in Alexandria, Egypt.

The Doctrines of the Trinity and of Christ

Arius, a presbyter in Alexandria, was preaching from the Bible, with Proverbs 8:22 as a central verse, that the Son is not eternal with the Father but is created by the Father. That verse, which attributes the first-person pronoun to "wisdom," reads as follows: "The LORD brought me forth as the first of his works, before his deeds of old." Arius and his followers argued their doctrine from this verse, which speaks of the creation of wisdom, and from the common early Christian understanding of Christ as "wisdom' (1 Cor 1:24, 30). These verses, these errant teachers said, subordinate Christ, the Son, to the Father, who alone is God and who had begotten—that is, *created*—a Son. Other passages they pointed to in support of their view were Psalm 45:7-8 and Isaiah 1:2 and the words "only begotten" in John 1:14, 18. Thus, according to Arius, it was not true to say "Always God, always Son" or "At the same time Father, at the same time Son," meaning that God the Father and God the Son are co-eternal and both possess the quality of deity.[1] Rather, Arius proclaimed that "before [the Son] was begotten or created or defined or established, he was not for he was not unbegotten" and that "the Son has a beginning, but God is without beginning." For Arius, the Son is a creature and is not eternal.

Arius's heresy brought forth the theological rebuttal of Alexander, bishop of Alexandria. Because of the havoc and schism it caused within the empire, it eventually led to Constantine's calling the First Ecumenical Council in Nicaea (in modern-day Turkey) during the winter of 324–325. Being "ecumenical," the synod's decision would be binding on the church throughout the world. The critical concern was the Son's essence and his relationship to the Father. The participants in the debate included principally the church's bishops but also Christian thinkers of nonepiscopal rank. In the end, on June 19, 325, the Nicene Creed affirmed that the Son shared the Father's divine nature.

> We believe in one God, Father, all-sovereign, maker of all things seen and unseen; and in one Lord Jesus Christ, the Son of God, begotten from the Father as only-begotten, that is, from the substance of the Father, God from God, light from light, true God from true God, begotten, not made, *homoousios* [Greek for "of the same essence"], one in, with the Father, through whom all things came to existence, the things in heaven and the things on earth, who because of men and our salvation came down and was incarnated, made man, suffered, and arose on the third day, ascended into heaven, comes to judge the living and the dead; and in one Holy Spirit. And those who say "there was once when he was not" or "he was not before he was begotten" or "he came into existence from nothing" or who affirm that the Son of God is of another *hypostasis* [Greek, "nature"] or substance, or a creature, or mutable or subject to change, such ones the catholic and apostolic church pronounces accursed and separated from the church.[2]

As a result, Arius was exiled and so were others who shared or were sympathetic with his views. Despite his doctrinal error, though, the bishops of the eastern region of the empire reestablished him in the church ten years later. Had he not died in 336, he would have regained his place among the pastors of Alexandria. However, Arianism remained a challenge to the orthodoxy of Nicaea into at least the last quarter of the fourth century.

Athanasius of Alexandria—who was a deacon from 311 to 328, during the early years of the Arian controversy—succeeded Alexander as bishop in 328. He was one of the church's finest theologians. Two of his writings are important to mention. In the first work, *On the Incarnation,* he developed from Scripture the key understanding of salvation as humanity's re-creation through the death and resurrection of Jesus Christ, the Word of God. Through his death the incarnate (human) Word took on himself humanity's God-appointed destiny of defeat by death. Through his resurrection the glorified, incorruptible, incarnate (human) Word renewed and recreated immortal humanity's corruptible, fallen nature. Athanasius said salvation is the renewal of our human nature, in all its features, material and immaterial (spirit and body), into the full, glorious image of God. God the Word (Jesus Christ) became human to renew what was human, to sanctify humanity through intimate unity with God. Salvation is not the salvation of humans to some nonhuman condition, to some mystical, intangible state. It is the salvation of humans in the sense that our human nature is retrieved from death and corruption by the One who shared our corruptible nature unto death and renewed it to immortality in his resurrection. Many of Paul's teachings reveal this close connection between the humanity of the Word of God and the salvation of our humanity.

> The gift is not like the trespass. For if the many died by the trespass of the one man [Adam] how much more did God's grace and the gift that came by the grace of the *one man,* Jesus Christ, overflow to the many! (Rom 5:15, italics added)

> For if, by the trespass of the one man [Adam], death reigned through that one man, how much more will those who receive God's abundant provision of grace and of the gift of righteousness reign in life through the *one man,* Jesus Christ. (Rom 5:17, italics added)

> For just as through the disobedience of the man [Adam] the many were made sinners, so also through the obedience of the

one man [Jesus Christ] the many will be made righteous. (Rom 5:19, italics added)

For since death came through a man [Adam], the resurrection of the dead comes also through *a man*. For as in Adam all die, so in Christ all will be made alive. (1 Cor 15:21-22, italics added)

For there is one God and one mediator between God and men, *the man* Christ Jesus, who gave himself as a ransom for all men—the testimony given in its proper time. (1 Tim 2:5-6, italics added)

By uniting his deity with our humanity, the eternal Word of God defeated death and raised the humanity of those who believe in him to the sure hope of immortal glory.

A second writing of Athanasius worth noting is his *Against the Arians.* From this important work one argument stands out: God alone can initiate and accomplish salvation. Therefore the Word of God, who became flesh, could not be a creature, as Arius asserted, but he must be of one substance with the Father—that is, he must fully share the "Godness" of the Father. Athanasius's *Against the Arians* became the classic rebuttal to Arianism.

The Second Ecumenical Council, held in Constantinople in 381, filled out what the Council of Nicaea had left unsaid about the Holy Spirit. Convened by Emperor Theodosius I to unify the Christian faith (and thereby important elements of the empire) against the subordination of the Son or Spirit to the Father, 150 church leaders agreed on two pivotal ideas. First, they ratified, with minor alterations, the Creed of Nicaea. Second, they added a statement on the Holy Spirit, which declared him one in substance with the Father and Son. Although this creed, known as the Creed of Constantinople, was not officially received until its reading at the Council of Chalcedon seventy years later, in 451, it accurately reflects the faith of the council in 381. The addition concerning the Spirit reads:

And [we believe] in the Holy spirit,
the Lord and life-giver,
who proceeds from the Father,
who is worshiped and glorified together
with the Father and Son,
who spoke through the prophets.[3]

By 381 the church had decided that the biblical words *begotten, Son, proceeds* and *Spirit* do not indicate a difference of substance or essence among the Father, the Son and the Spirit. They all share deity, "Godness," fully and equally.

Three theologians who helped Christians in the latter half of the fourth century think more clearly about the trinitarian God are known as the Cappadocians: Basil of Caesarea, Gregory of Nyssa and Gregory of Nazianzus. They emphasized God's unity of essence along with his eternal existence as three persons. The language chosen to communicate this mysterious, yet biblically revealed and therefore necessarily binding concept of the Christian God, was "One *ousia* [Greek for 'substance' or 'essence'] and three *hypostases* [Greek taken to mean 'persons']." In one of his letters Basil expressed the soundness of the church's faith in this way:

> If we have no distinct perception of the separate characteristics, namely, fatherhood, sonship, and sanctification, but form our conception of God from the general idea of existence, we cannot possibly give a sound account of our faith. We must, therefore, confess the faith by adding the particular to the common. The Godhead is common; the fatherhood particular. We must therefore combine the two and say, "I believe in God the Father." The like course must be pursued in the confession of the Son; we must combine the particular with the common and say, "I believe in God the Son." So in the case of the Holy Spirit we must make our utterance conform to the appellation and say, "I believe also in the divine Holy Spirit." Hence it results that there is a satisfactory preservation of the unity by the confession of the one Godhead, while in the distinction of the individual

properties regarded in each other there is the confession of the peculiar properties of the Persons.[4]

After the leaders of the church developed and expressed the trinitarian faith, they next turned their theological skills to the question of the person of Christ. The Son, they knew, was one in essence with the Father and the Spirit. But how were they to understand God the Son's relationship to humanity in the incarnation? What did it mean for the Word to become flesh (Jn 1:14)? Two or three answers were offered, all of which the church ultimately found unacceptable. This led to the Fourth Ecumenical Council at Chalcedon in 451.

One unacceptable model of the relationship between the deity and flesh of Jesus Christ is known as Word-flesh Christology, associated with Apollinarius of Laodicea (ca. 315–393). In his understanding the divine Word replaced the human spirit, soul and mind in Jesus so that the flesh was the only human element Jesus possessed. In this way Apollinarius emphasized the unity of Christ's person: Christ was a divine, immaterial center controlling and guiding outward human, physical flesh. Christ was the Word become *flesh* but not the Word become *human.* Apollinarius sacrificed the humanity of Christ for the unity of Christ's person.

Another view the church rejected was the Christology associated with Nestorius, bishop of Constantinople (ca. 381–451). Although perhaps wrongly attributed to Nestorius, the view has traditionally been called Nestorianism, or Word-human Christology. Nestorianism, in contrast to Apollinarianism, emphasized the fullness of both the Word's deity and his humanity. But it emphasized them to such a degree that Christ was spoken of as almost two persons: one divine and one human, the Word of God and the human Jesus. Nestorianism sacrificed the unity of Christ's person for the fullness of deity and humanity.

The church also found a third model of Christology unacceptable: Eutychianism. Again, it is not totally clear that the one charged with promoting this view actually believed it, but it is traditionally linked with him. Eutyches, head of a monastery in Constantinople in the middle of the fifth century, confessed two natures before the incarnation but only one after the incarnation. This was understood to teach that the human nature had been absorbed by the divine nature.

Although all these views were ultimately insufficient, they were all attempts to understand the biblical revelation concerning Christ's person and the relationship between his deity and humanity. After Nicaea, the church confessed that the Word of God, God's Son, was of one substance with the Father's "Godness"—in other words, that the Son is deity. But what does John 1:14 mean by saying that God the Word "became flesh"? Did it mean that he just appeared to be human? Did it mean that he was just flesh, skin, bones, blood and organs, not fully human with a human mind, soul and spirit? Did it mean that he had simply assumed a human nature but that the human and divine remained separate? Did it mean that now there were actually two Beings, one who did divine, Godlike things (healing people, walking on water, raising dead people to life) and another who did weak, humanlike things (sleeping, eating, being tired, dying)? At the Fourth Ecumenical Council of Chalcedon the church rejected all such interpretations of John 1:14. (The third council, mentioned briefly below, was held twenty years earlier in Ephesus.)

This is, after all, what church leaders do. They explain to their congregations acceptable parameters within which they are to understand and interpret the Bible. They also point out unacceptable interpretations. Good theology doesn't just happen. Church leaders who care for their congregations don't allow unacceptable thinking about the Trinity and Christ's person to go unchecked. What one thinks about Christ's person or God really matters. As A. W. Tozer said:

What comes into our minds when we think about God is the most important thing about us. . . . For this reason the gravest question before the church is always God himself, and the most portentous fact about any man is not what he at any given time may say or do, but what he in his heart conceives God to be like. . . . Before the Christian church goes into eclipse anywhere there must first be a corrupting of her simple basic theology. She simply gets a wrong answer to the question, "What is God like?" and goes on from there.[5]

This wrong answer applies to both the congregation's view of God as Trinity and to its view about God the Son's incarnation. Church leaders must first be the church's theologians. Knowing this, the church leaders at Chalcedon delivered to the church this great statement about Christ our Lord:

Following, therefore, the holy fathers, we confess one and the same Son, who is our Lord Jesus Christ, and we all agree in teaching that this very same Son is complete in his deity and complete—the very same—in his humanity, truly God and truly a human being, this very same one being composed of rational soul and a body, co-essential with the Father as to his deity, and co-essential with us—the very same one—as to his humanity, being like us in every respect apart from sin. As to his deity, he was born from the Father before the ages, but as to his humanity, the very same one was born in the last days from the Virgin Mary, the Mother of God, for our sake and the sake of our salvation: one and the same Christ, Son, Lord, Only Begotten, acknowledged to be unconfusedly, unalterably, undividedly, inseparably in two natures, since the difference of the natures is not destroyed because of the union, but on the contrary, the character of each nature is preserved and comes together in one person and one hypostasis, not divided or torn into two persons but one and the same Son and only-begotten God, Logos, Lord Jesus Christ—just as in earlier times the prophets and also the Lord Jesus Christ Himself taught us about Him, and the symbol of our Fathers transmitted to us.[6]

This Chalcedonian Creed emphasizes the oneness of Christ's person and the distinction of his full two natures, divine and human, in unity with each other. Against the Apollinarians, it teaches that Christ had a human soul in addition to human flesh. Against the Nestorians, it teaches that Christ's two natures are distinct yet not divided or separable. Against the Eutychians, it taught that Christ was of the same human essence as we are and that both of his natures (human and divine) exist without either being absorbed by the other.

Sometimes the creed's reference to Mary as "Mother of God" *(Theotokos)* is troublesome to Protestants. But the phrase was fundamentally christological, included to defeat the view of Nestorius. The great theologian Cyril of Alexandria had introduced it against the Nestorian heresy at the Third Ecumenical Council of Ephesus in 431. The point is that we can't merely refer to the child born to Mary as "that human baby." Mary's son is also, even in the humility of birth, *God* the Son. Therefore, as the woman who birthed *God* the Son when he became human, Mary is rightly, in that sense, the mother of God, the one of whom God incarnate was born. It says nothing of Mary as God's Creator or Life-giver.

Do the councils of Nicaea, Constantinople and Chalcedon answer all our questions about the Trinity and the incarnation? No. But they do give us boundaries within which we find acceptable interpretations of the Scriptures about the Trinity and the two natures of Christ. We may not have all the answers, but we know things we *should* say and believe and we know views we *shouldn't* hold. Mature Christians may be more than those who know and confess true doctrine, but they can never be less.

The Practice of Monasticism

"Christians found many ways to express their separation."[7] So wrote Martin Marty in his helpful little book *A Short History of*

Christianity, under his brief treatment of monasticism. He added that "for some, holiness was to be found in the attempt at complete isolation and removal from the world."[8]

Arising in the latter part of the third century and finding more concrete expression within the fourth, the monastic movement took various paths of asceticism in both solitary life and community. The hermits, or anchorites, retreated early to the desert of Egypt, where they struggled against the forces of darkness through constant prayer, fasting, reading and reciting of the Bible, and manual labor. Though given to isolation, the hermits often practiced their ascetic lifestyle in common areas. An early leader was Antony of Egypt. In Syria the hermitic life would at times embrace some extremes not practiced elsewhere. For example, one Syrian ascetic, Simon the Stylite, sat atop a high column for thirty years, praying, preaching and offering counsel to those who came to observe him.

However, not all monks were religious recluses. Communities of monks, traced back in Egypt to Pachomius, also developed. All their property was held in common; the monks practiced spiritual disciplines regularly; they worked and they submitted to a hierarchical structure of authority. Communal monastic life, called cenobitism, also found root throughout Asia Minor. Basil of Caesarea, one of the Cappadocians mentioned earlier in the discussion of the trinitarian controversy, was an influential organizer and leader, even producing a set of rules. He emphasized the need for those in the monastery to minister to the needs of people in the towns and cities. Education, hospitality and medical care were viewed as corollaries of the contemplative life.

In the West, throughout Italy, modern-day France, Belgium, Germany and Spain, monastic communities and some hermitic ascetics practiced their understanding of the spiritual life. The classical Western expression developed in the sixth century with Benedict of Nursia's *Rule.* Drawing from other monastic rules, Benedict composed his own list for his cenobite monastery in Monte Cassino, Italy. His *Rule* emphasized obedience to the communal leader (the abbot), balanced the ascetic life with communal charity and centered the monk's day around communal praise, manual labor and Bible reading. The monastery was not to be totally reclusive from society; it was also to provide a ministry of teaching.

The monastic movement must be understood in the context of the Christian quest for holiness, separation and discipleship. Often viewed by modern-day Christians with skepticism, monasticism continues to puzzle contemporary minds. This is unfortunate, for although perhaps somewhat extreme in some practices, Christian monasticism was fueled by a drive to be Christ's disciples, to enter victoriously into spiritual warfare and to flee from "friendship with the world" (Jas 4:4). In a way, monasticism replaced martyrdom as the supreme expression of discipleship. In a culture in which Christianity was now welcome and even sanctioned, Christians were no longer called to reject conformity to the religion and society of Rome but to reject conformity with a world grown complacent, presumptuous and casual about following Christ. The monks sought to imitate Christ in self-denial, an imitation for which their reading of Scripture helped prepare them.

Douglas Burton-Christie, an expert on the use of the Bible within the monastic movement, has described their attachment to the Bible in this way: "The Scriptures were experienced as authoritative words which pierced the hearts of the monks, illuminated them concerning the central issues of their lives, protected and comforted them during dark times of struggle and anxiety, and provided practical help in their ongoing quest for holiness."[9] Burton-Christie cites the monk Antony, who told his students, "Whatever you *do* you should always *have* before you the testimony of Scripture."[10]

To monastery residents, the Bible was not merely to be read;

it was to be appropriated. For them, understanding had not occurred until the passage had been internalized, until transformation of life had taken place. When a monk obeyed the Scriptures, then he understood them.

The monks' commitment to silence and isolation was an attempt to obey Paul's command to "pray without ceasing" (1 Thess 5:17 KJV), even in manual labor. Such commitment was also an attempt to take seriously the Bible's teaching regarding care in speech, the destructive power of words, the inseparable connection between the heart and the tongue, the call to live out what one says one believes (Ps 39:1-2; Prov 18:21; Mt 12:33-34; 23:3). Silence was preferred to foolishness; a quiet tongue was preferred to a malicious one; the absence of speech in contemplation of holiness was far better than wicked words. They believed that when a person's heart is bloated with evil, it is best for that person to keep his mouth closed.

The monks, however, were not naive about their practice of silence. The early church father Poemen agreed that silence was a wonderful virtue. "But," he cautioned, "people who hold their tongues should not always account themselves silent. If their minds are occupied with their neighbor's shortcomings, their silence is as bad as senseless chattering."[11] In other words, we may not be speaking evil, but that doesn't mean we're not thinking evil.

The monks' renunciation of earthly possessions was biblically informed too. Renunciation imitated Christ and the disciples and followed Christ's teachings (Mt 4:20; 6:25-33; 8:18-22; 19:21, 27). The need for detachment from earthly goods is stated in a number of ways in the Scriptures. The psalmist wrote, "Cast your cares on the LORD and he will sustain you" (Ps 55:22). Paul stated, "We brought nothing into the world, and we can take nothing out of it" (1 Tim 6:7). Job affirmed, "The LORD gave and the LORD has taken away" (Job 1:21). So devoted were they to the Scriptures as the foundation of their spiritual lives

that the monks under Benedict's *Rule* sang all 150 psalms every
week!

Before we leave the monks, let's listen to several selections
from their rich deposit of writings on the spiritual life:

Two old men lived together for many years without a quarrel.
One said to the other: "Let us have one quarrel with each other,
as is the way of men." And the other answered: "I do not know
how a quarrel happens." And the first said: "Look, I put a tile
between us, and I say, That's mine. Then you say, No, it's mine.
That is how you begin a quarrel." So they put a tile between
them, and one of them said: "That's mine." And the other said:
"No, it's mine." And he answered: "Yes, it is yours. Take it away."
And they went away unable to argue with each other.[12]

An old man said to a brother: "When a proud or vain thought
enters you, examine your conscience to see if you are keeping
God's commandments; if you love your enemies; if you rejoice
in your adversary's triumph, and are grieved at his downfall; if
you know yourself to be an unprofitable servant, and a sinner
beyond all others. But not even then must you think yourself to
have corrected all your faults; knowing that this thought alone
in you shall undo all the other good you have done."[13]

Abba Hyperichius said: "The tree of life is lofty, and humility
climbs in it."[14]

A Syrian solitary [a monk living as a hermit] came to him [Poe-
men] once lamenting the hardness of his heart. "Read the Word
of God," said Poemen; "the drip of a fountain pierces the stone,
and the gentle word falling softly day by day on the dead hard
heart after a while infallibly melts it."[15]

"What is a living faith?" was a question put to Poemen one day.
"A living faith," he answered, "consists in thinking little of one-
self, and showing tenderness towards others."[16]

Another of his [Poemen's] sayings: "A warm heart, boiling with
charity to God and man, is not tormented with temptations; they

swarm round a cold one. You see no flies hovering about the caldron boiling on the fire. Set it down and let it grow cold, and it is black with flies."[17]

And from the *Rule of Saint Benedict* comes this statement about prayer: "If we want to ask a favor of any person of power, we presume not to approach but with humility and respect. How much more ought we to address ourselves to the Lord and God of all things with a humble and entire devotion? We are not to imagine that our prayers shall be heard because we use many words, but because the heart is pure and the spirit penitent."[18]

The second part of this book, which treats the story of the church in the Middle Ages, or medieval period, will continue this glimpse into the history of Christian spirituality. We will see it in splendor and in darkness.

Part 2

Emeralds
The Church in the Middle Ages

Art reveals much about the values of a particular age. Let's take a tour of some symbols of the beliefs of some medieval Christians.[1] First, as we enter a church, we encounter several woodcarvings on the ends of benches in the shape of battle shields. A commonplace in the Christian art of the Middle Ages, these shields reminded the faithful of the Passion of our Lord. On each shield is chiseled an emblem of the Passion narrative. On one is the crown of thorns; on another, the three nails; on a third, the hammer; the fourth holds the sponge on a rod; the fifth, the dice. As we walk through the church, continuing to glance at the benches, we see the spear, the whip, Judas's hand with a bag of silver, the cock that crowed. Our brothers and sisters in the Middle Ages never tired of telling the story of our Lord's betrayal, crucifixion and death. It was the basis of their salvation.

At another church we are held captive by the glasswork. Represented in the glass are acts of mercy taken from Jesus' words in Matthew 25:35-36. One depicts a believer feeding the hungry as he distributes bread from a basket. A second shows the same person filling the bowls of the thirsty with water. Another shows a Christian holding clothes for five men who are without adequate covering. The last one represents three prisoners, feet in stocks, being visited by the benefactor. These artworks show what is best in medieval Christianity: a focus on the shame and suffering of Christ and the Christian duty to follow him in a life of merciful service to the needy.

As we saw in part one, the jewelers of the early church set and produced some lovely diamond pieces for our treasure collection of perspective building in our day. But believers in the Middle Ages, from 500 to about 1500, contributed fine emerald ornaments as well. Their concerns differed from those of the earlier church, but some practices were the same, such as self-denial in worship and discipleship.

People in the Middle Ages were faced with the problems that can occur when a "Christian culture" is confused with conversion of the heart, when institutions and hierarchies are confused with church and leadership, and when theology is of concern to the clergy but not the laity. But in the Middle Ages we can also gaze on brilliant examples of Christian leadership, prayer, the right use of the mind and the practice of the devotional life.

3

Empires, Emperors & Pastors

IN CHAPTER TWO WE BRIEFLY DISCUSSED the christological controversy, the Council of Chalcedon and monasticism of the fifth century. That century was a turbulent one for the Roman Empire. In that century the Germanic tribes invaded the empire, Rome was sacked and the Roman Empire fell.

Toward the end of the third century the Roman Empire was almost fragmented by German and Persian attacks. Then in the fourth and early fifth centuries the empire had to give attention to defending its many frontiers. In the south the frontiers extended across the Mediterranean Sea to the desert edges of North Africa. In the west the empire extended to the coasts of Portugal and Spain. In the north the empire extended across the English Channel to just above the river Tyne in England (exclusive of Scotland and Ireland). In central Europe the Roman Empire extended to the Danube and Rhine rivers in central and southeastern Europe (including Spain, France, Belgium, Switzerland, Italy, Yugoslavia, Bulgaria and Greece). The

Germanic tribes threatened this frontier. The eastern frontier, threatened by the Persians and Arabs, lay just east of the Black Sea, proceeding southward to enclose Syria, Israel and the Sinai Peninsula against the Mediterranean. And by the end of the fourth century (A.D. 395) the empire was divided between the two sons of Theodosius I into the Western and Eastern Roman Empire, with the line of division running north to south between the heel of Italy and the western coast of Greece.

The Fall of the Empire, the Rise of a Christian Culture

Unable to protect all frontiers at once and experiencing inner turmoil, the Western empire weakened and so, almost by default, the Eastern portion gained strength. Then at the very end of 406 it happened: the Germanic invasion of the West began. Sometimes more migration than military conquest, the invasion involved different tribes of different character with different relations to Christianity. One tribe, the Vandals, who ended up finally in North Africa (around 430–533), also carried out the devastating sack of Rome in 455. The Ostrogoths made their way to Italy, where they ruled from 490 to 536. Another group, the Visigoths, sacked Rome in 410 and then proceeded to Spain, which they occupied until the Muslims claimed it at the beginning of the eighth century. The Franks occupied northern Gaul (France) from around 500, and in 532 they conquered the Burgundians, who had settled in southern Gaul. All these tribes, except the Franks, had embraced Christianity to some degree, holding to the Arian heresy. Looming in the future was the threat from the Arabs who, with the rise of Islam, eventually occupied Spain (starting about 711) and even probed into southern France. Christianity in the West was intimidated by the Arabs and was fragmented by barbarians and Arians.

In such a world, missionary endeavors to the Germanic barbarians and Arians, as well as to those outside the Western continent, became both obedience to Christ's call and a political necessity. A ruler who was converted to orthodox Christianity might treat the conquered peoples more compassionately than others would. At times, regrettably, the gospel deteriorated into an argument for God's power over the pagan gods. Apparent conversions sometimes looked like that of Clovis, king of the Franks. In the midst of a battle that he was losing, Clovis cried out, "Christ Jesus . . . I have invoked my own gods, and they have withdrawn from me. . . . Thee . . . I [now] invoke; if Thou give me victory . . . if I find in Thee power . . . I will believe in Thee, and will be baptized in Thy name."[1] Victory and material prosperity were seen as indicators of supernatural power.

This approach—assenting that the Christian God is superior to another god because of temporal, earthly blessings—was entirely at odds with humility and shame. It led some to true faith in Christ and others to a mere religious formalism. The latter merely embraced Christianity as a superior culture or power. This formalism increased as in future generations the idea of Christianity as a more beautiful and powerful society than the barbaric one became a more controlling notion. This seemed natural because the superior elements of Roman civilization accompanied the entrance of Christianity into various lands. With Theodosius' naming of Christianity as the official religion, the sheer numbers of *apparent* conversions also contributed to such formalism.

This is a danger seen repeatedly throughout the history of Christianity. The dynamic works like this: A "Christian" culture develops with its own way of dressing, its own way of talking, its own art, its own music, its own everything. Over time, unfortunately, conforming to the "Christian" culture becomes confused with Christian conversion. If one becomes a member of the culture, practicing the distinctives of the group, one is acknowledged as converted, even if there has been no supernatural intervention of the Holy Spirit. Because of the union between Christianity and Roman civilization, at times it was difficult to tell the two apart.

The mass "conversion" of people in the early Middle Ages, along with the controlling idea of a society of the baptized, posed a problem for theologians and pastors: how explicitly did a baptized member of the church have to know and understand the Christian faith?[2] It was assumed that baptism at infancy placed a person irretrievably among the faithful. The one baptized already possessed the essential component of "faith," and growth in explicit knowledge of the doctrines of the faith was not required. The essence of Christian identity had become inseparably linked to the baptism of infants; those who were baptized were viewed as having "implicit" faith although they might be ignorant of doctrinal particulars.

Pursuing knowledge and understanding of the faith was the task of churchmen, the theologians. The people, it was assumed, knew or should know the doctrines only roughly, and this they picked up in formal worship. This view of things introduced into Christian thinking the idea that doctrine or specific knowledge of important theological issues was the arena of theologians, not of "simple" laypersons. The simple folk had faith even if they didn't know or couldn't articulate what they believed. Church leaders reasoned that laypersons couldn't be expected to know theology.

John Calvin, hundreds of years in the future, would present a different view. He argued that faith has knowledge, not ignorance, for its foundation. Faith that obtains salvation *knows* God to be the merciful Father who reconciles us to himself through Christ, who is *known* as our righteousness. For Calvin, faith and understanding are joined.[3]

Yes, in the Middle Ages the lines between politics and gospel, formalism and faith, society and church, culture and conversion became blurred at times. These tensions strained against each other repetitively, sometimes climactically. But within those blurred moments the spiritual life of the church continued. A tendency to criticize the church of the Middle Ages excessively may say more about our blindness to our own blurrings and tensions than anything else.

Despite the church's fumbles within a disintegrating world, believers during the medieval period still sought to live according to God's Word. "The Bible was the most studied book of the Middle Ages. Bible study represented the highest branch of learning." So wrote Beryl Smalley in her acclaimed classic *The Study of the Bible in the Middle Ages*.[4] And Benedicta Ward has written similarly, "Medieval devotion to God was based on the Latin Bible, the Sacred Scriptures, heard, read, or seen."[5] We see evidence of this, for instance, in a sermon of one medieval Christian, Aelred of Rievaulx. Concerning the power of Scripture to console, he wrote, "Brothers, however cast down we may be by harassment or heartache, the consolations of Scripture will lift us up again, for all the things that were written in former days were written for our instruction so that we, through the steadfastness and encouragement the Scriptures give us, might have hope. I tell you, brothers, no misfortune can touch us, no situation so galling or distressing can arise that does not as soon as Holy Writ seizes hold of us, either fade into nothingness or become bearable."[6]

Sadly, the central role of the Bible in the life of medieval believers has not always been recognized, and the Christianity of the medieval church has often been judged as decrepit and corrupted, as a religious view not built on reflection on the Bible. Certain abuses of the papacy, the Crusades, the struggles among emperor, king and pope, disease, war, invasion, aspects of suffocating sacramentalism and some unsatisfactory views on the doctrine of salvation have left most modern-day Protestants with a bad taste for medieval Christianity. For many Christians today, gloom, superstition and vain piety, rather than joy, faith and love as fruit of the Spirit, seem to capture the essence of religious practice in that era. Thus we hear the popular yet pejorative nickname for the period: the Dark Ages.

But what were the lives of devoted believers actually like in the Middle Ages? What were they seeing in the Bible, and how was it influencing their life and worship?

Gregory the Great

Gregory I, also known as Gregory the Great, was elected from his quiet life as a monk to be the bishop of Rome, the pope, in 590. A skilled administrator and statesman, Gregory also possessed a vision faithful to the Great Commission. In the period of his papacy he pioneered successful missionary endeavors to Spain and England and meditated deeply on the Bible. Delighted yet humbled by Scripture, he said that it was "like a river, shallow and deep, in which lambs can walk and elephants swim."[7] A man of enduring humility, pastoral sensitivity and moral strength, Gregory introduces us to Christian devotion in early medieval Europe. Bernard McGinn has noted, "As his *Moralia on Job* [a commentary on the moral life from the book of Job] shows, the pope's major concern was not with speculation on the metaphysical implications of Christianity, but with the practical application on belief in the great mysteries, especially of Christ and the church, for individual behavior."[8]

We have already spoken of martyrdom in early Christianity and of the way in which early monasticism attempted to embrace martyrdom's emphasis on the life of discipleship. In some of his homilies Gregory helps us gain yet another perspective. Though a monk himself, Gregory preached in these homilies an understanding of martyrdom as "spiritual martyrdom," which he believed should be undertaken by all the faithful in times of peace.[9] Concluding a sermon that recounted and honored the life of a mother whose seven sons fell to martyrdom, he told his audience, "Our Redeemer, dearly beloved, died out of love for us; let us learn to conquer ourselves out of love for him. . . . This is not a time of persecution, yet our peace also has its martyrdom. Even if we do not submit our necks to the metal sword, still we are putting to death the carnal desires in our hearts with a spiritual sword."[10]

Putting to death carnality, which he called spiritual martyrdom, particularly involves love for others, both friends and enemies, and patience. This is because actual martyrdom requires these same virtues. Therefore, concerning love, Gregory preached this:

> No one is persecuting us to the point of death. How then can we prove that we love our friends? But there is something we should do during times of peace in the Church to make clear whether we are strong enough to die for the sake of our loving during times of persecution. John, the author of this gospel says: He who has this world's goods and sees his brother in need and closes the heart against him, how does God's love dwell in him? And John the Baptist says: Let him who has two tunics give to him who has none. Will a person, then, who will not give up his tunic for the sake of God during quiet times give up his life during a persecution? Cultivate the virtue of love in tranquil times by showing mercy, then, so that it will be unconquerable in times of disorder. Learn first to give up your possessions for almighty God, and then for yourself.[11]

In speaking to the faithful about patience in light of the patient martyr Mennas, Gregory said these words: "If with the Lord's help we are striving to observe the virtue of patience, though we are living in a time of peace for the Church, yet we are holding the palm of martyrdom. There are in truth two kinds of martyrdom: one in the heart, the other in heart and action at the same time. And so we can be martyrs, even when we are not slain by anyone's sword. To die at the hands of a persecutor is unmistakably martyrdom; to bear insults, to love one who hates us, is martyrdom on our secret thought."[12]

These writings show that the faithful devotion of the early martyrs, a devotion in imitation of Christ, continued to serve as a model for discipleship in times of peace. But besides providing a model for the monastics, Gregory's sermons show us that in the Middle Ages all believers were called to imitate Christ in the key virtues that undergird the commitment to actual death, namely, love and patience.

Gregory also had a rich concept of the ministerial office.[13] Pastors, according to Gregory, were to preach so that their people embraced righteousness. In this spirit we can appreciate Gregory's various metaphors for preaching and for the preacher's listeners. Preaching is a rain that waters; it is arrows that pierce the listeners' hearts; it is sparks that burst into flame on the hearts they touch. Gregory likened the audience to the strings of a musical instrument. The preacher must play them, plucking them each differently, and must realize that his words will not fall the same way on each ear. For Gregory, eloquence in preaching stemmed not only from exegesis and rhetoric but also from the preacher's inner life, a humble, contemplative love for God and disdain for the world: "He who thinks about his own life inwardly and edifies others outwardly, instructing them by his own example, dips the pen of his tongue, as it were, in his heart, and writes outwardly with his hand in words for his neighbor."[14] Furthermore, any teaching or homily was ultimately dependent on the Holy Spirit. Preaching on John 14:26, Gregory said, "It is justly promised that *'He will teach you all things,'* because unless the Spirit is present in the heart of a listener, the teacher's utterance is useless. No one should attribute to this teacher what he understands from him, because unless there is an inner teacher, the one outside is exerting himself in vain."[15]

In Gregory's teaching, the holy man does not covet authoritarian control, but in service to God he shepherds the flock.[16] Such leaders never feel secure from the treachery of their evil yearnings. They are inwardly, authentically still and tranquil when chaos erupts. Instead of responding in anger to the hatred of enemies, they pray. They do not answer abuse with abuse. In adversity they are, with apparent naiveté, warm, sweet and simple.

In his classic *Book of Pastoral Rule,* Gregory outlined the characteristics he believed should mark the Christian minister. These characteristics are not penned by a Christian mind covered with gloom, as our stereotype of the Middle Ages would have it; rather, they are the words of one enlightened by Scripture.

> The ruler should always be pure in thought.
>
> The ruler should always be chief in action, that by his living he may point out the way of life to those that are put under him.
>
> The ruler should be discreet in keeping silence, profitable in speech; lest he either utter what ought to be suppressed or suppress what he ought to utter.
>
> The ruler should be a near neighbor to every one in sympathy.
>
> The ruler should be, through humility, a companion of good livers, and through the zeal of righteousness, rigid against the vices of evildoers.
>
> The ruler also ought to understand how commonly vices pass themselves off as virtues.
>
> [The ruler should] be inspired by the spirit of heavenly fear and love [and] meditate daily on the precepts of Sacred Writ.[17]

The Pope, the Church and the Ruler (Part 1)

As the kings and lords of the various territories in Europe converted to orthodox Christianity (usually followed in conversion by the lower classes whom they ruled), there developed, in the eighth and ninth centuries, a significant relationship between church and ruler. The ruler had complete control over lands and property, and being Christian, he felt obligated to provide a parish for his people. The ruler was therefore the authority over the parish, and the area over which he exercised jurisdiction was a spiritual community. Informed by the Old Testament concept of kingship, which unified civil, military and religious offices, the Germanic kings became central to the church. The just king was expected to defend strangers, chastise adulterers, protect churches, cherish the poor with alms, trust God in all things, believe in God according to the catholic (one, true, universal) faith and attend to prayers at the hours fixed.[18] If a king failed in this calling, then on the basis of the story of Solomon's fall and the split of his kingdom (1 Kings 11:11-13), the king was warned that he might experience the enslavement of his people, deaths of loved ones, enemy invasions, destruction of herds and flocks, disasters from the weather and the end of his dynasty.

The bishops, too, rose in power because of the lack of local stability left by the Roman Empire's disintegration. They represented God, and the people recognized them as leaders. Not all of them, however, lived godly lives. Some were greedy and had attained their diocese through purchase. Others demanded payment for their ministry and lived in immorality. Such corruption led to decline in the laity's interest in spiritual things. Nevertheless, bishops served as feudal lords, as spiritual guides and priests, and as advisers to kings. They owned real estate and exercised some control over public opinion. They were responsible to fulfill their feudal duties to the king. Rulers, however, found themselves also in submission to the bishops. As a ruler, the king appointed his bishop. Yet as a Christian (and at times a wise politician), the king bowed to the bishop and was crowned by him. Following the Old Testament practice of anointing kings, the act of coronation enhanced the authority of both kings and church. Ultimately, however, it delivered to medieval Christianity the notion of Christendom as a unity of the secular and the sacred, the civil and the ecclesial.

A central moment in this relationship came on Christmas Day, 800, when Pope Leo III crowned the king of France—Charles the Great, or Charlemagne (ca. 742–814)—as the Roman (Western) emperor. Two events precipitated this act: Charlemagne had accumulated extensive dominions in the west and the pope had promised to protect Charlemagne. The coronation recognized Charlemagne's achievements and sealed the pope's promise. Because of the coronation, Charlemagne, as the recognized protector of the church, its guardian and benefactor, experienced a new depth of unity between church and ruler. Charlemagne took his responsibility to the church seriously and instituted quality control within clerical offices and monasteries and eradicated heresy. Charlemagne saw the clergy as the foundation to a society that existed for the service of God.

Such an interest in quality control within the monasteries was necessary in the ninth century and even more so in the tenth. Laxity and corruption, often connected to the monks' involvement in civil affairs and their integration into the feudal political system, entered monasteries more and more. The secular and the temporal increasingly interfered with the spiritual and the eternal. The Benedictine rule came to be honored less and less. This was harmful not only to the monasteries but also to the laity they served. As Vivian Greene has aptly stated, "For the laity the monastery was above all the power-house of prayer, its Masses and its daily offices a continuous chain of petition to God."[19] And this was the case for the entire society, not just the lower classes.

Kings even viewed monasteries as being "less centers of private religious exercise, than centers of public intercession and prayer" to serve the whole community.[20] While people worked the fields, the monks prayed for the workers' harvest. While the king governed and defended the kingdom, the monks prayed for security and peace. But this praying didn't occur if the monks were carousing.

Happily, wide-reaching reform took place in and through the monastery of Cluny in Burgundy, where strict observance of the Benedictine rule was restored and lay, secular rule was absent. It was under the sole supervision of ecclesiological authorities. Through the tenth and eleventh centuries a renaissance of spiritual discipline spread from Italy to Spain as other monasteries, with Cluny, returned to what they understood as the ideals of the early church. Celibacy and purity were restored, prayer was recaptured, worship was revived and lay secular supervision was rescinded. At the beginning of the next chapter, we will see what the monks' practice of prayer looked like. And we will continue our survey of Christian life and devotion in the Middle Ages.

4

Medieval
Lessons on
Prayer,
Thinking &
Devotion

A TRUE MONK EMBRACED A VISION of the spiritual life in anticipation of the life to come.[1] It was a life lived in tension between temporary existence in the present world and an indifference toward it. He envisioned himself as dead to the world and a despiser of earthly things, and though not a member of the majority of believers, he served the earthly community by his vision and set standards for it. The monastic way of life created conditions under which the monk could live in accord with the Lord's teaching to his disciples.

Monasticism and Prayer

Jesus' teachings on prayer (such as Luke 18:1: "they should always pray and not give up") and other scriptural commands concerning prayer were foremost in the monks' minds. We see this in the earliest moments of monastic history with the famous monk Antony. Athanasius of Alexandria tells us that Antony "prayed often, for he had learned that one should pray to the Lord without ceasing" (see 1 Thess 5:17).[2] Similarly, Bernard of Clairvaux wrote, "We must not devote ourselves to prayer once or twice, but frequently, diligently, letting God know the longings of our hearts and letting him hear, at times, the voice of our mouth. This is why it is said, 'Let your petitions be made known to God, (Phil 4:6)' which happens as a result of persistence and diligence in prayer."[3]

The populace valued the monk's lifestyle because through it other biblical teaching came to life. Through the intercessory prayer of a monk they embraced the words of James 5:16: "The prayer of a righteous man is powerful and effective." For instance, in a letter to the abbot Hugo of Cluny, Henry III petitioned Hugo to become his son's godfather: "Which man who knows the right way would not hope for your prayers and those of your monks? Who would not strive to hold fast to the indissoluble bond of your love, you whose prayer is all the purer in that it is remote from worldly deed, all the worthier in that it is near to God's sight?"[4]

If you have ever gone to a brother or sister in Christ, seeking that person's prayer support because of what you know about his or her purity and faithful prayer life, you understand Henry's viewpoint. The confidence and peace you had as a result of sharing your need with the brother or sister was the same sense of security the monks offered. Intercessory prayer, then, was central to the monk's ministry. In this way they ministered to the community and carried out part of their pastoral service. And this was part of the monk's focus: service. Following is the story of one such monk, Columba.

An Irishman's wife of the sixth century had taken an aversion to her husband (probably for good reason). When she went to the monk Columba for counsel, he reminded her of the Bible's teaching on the permanence of marriage.

She replied, "I am ready to do everything—except live with

him." She said she would be faithful to her domestic responsibilities. She said she would even leave for a convent. But she would not dwell with that man another minute!

The wise Columba replied that a convent was out of the question so long as her husband was alive. "But," he added, "let us fast and pray—you, your husband, and myself."

"Oh," said the woman, "I know that you can obtain even what is impossible from God."

All three then fasted, and Columba spent the entire night alert and awake in prayer. The next morning he gently approached the woman and with tender irony asked her to which convent she had decided to flee.

"To none," she replied. "My heart has been changed tonight. I know not how I have passed from hate to love." From that day on she lived with her husband lovingly and faithfully.[5]

In the monks' daily routine there were many scheduled times of prayer; the first time was at dawn. Their prayers demonstrated a deep dependence on God's grace, a confession of their mortality and a healthy fear of sin. Although they recited the majority of the liturgies in Latin, there exists an old English liturgy from around the tenth century. Note the poetic imagery of sun, illumination and darkness, which reflects on the light of the new day, and its overwhelming concern for purity:

> In the first hour of the day, that is at the sun's rising, we should praise God and eagerly pray him that he, out of his tenderness of heart, illumine our hearts with the illumination of the true Sun—that is, that he by his grace so illumine our inward thought that the devil may not through harmful darkness lead us astray from the right path nor too much impede us with the snares of sin. Be, Lord God, a noble helpmate; look, Lord, upon me, and help me quickly then in my mortal need.[6]

Such a beginning to each new day has scriptural support. David and the sons of Korah did something similar:

Give ear to my words, O LORD,
consider my sighing.
Listen to my cry for help,
    my King and my God,
    for to you I pray.
In the morning, O LORD, you hear my voice;
    in the morning I lay my request before you
    and wait in expectation. (Ps 5:1-3)

I cry to you for help, O LORD;
    in the morning prayer comes before you. (Ps 88:13)

The Features of Monastic Prayer:
Brevity, Purity and Constancy

What did the practice of early and medieval monastic prayer look like? From Scripture the monks determined that their prayers should be pure, brief, frequent and nurtured through the reading of Scripture. Since even in a monastery (let alone the rat race of the twenty-first century) distractions could be frequent (interruptions, wandering of the mind, worries, drowsiness), prayer done alone and in common with other monks was to be short in duration. The *Rule* of Saint Benedict says, "We are not to imagine that our prayers shall be heard because we use many words, but because the heart is pure and the spirit penitent. Therefore prayer must be short and pure, unless a feeling of divine inspiration prolong it. Prayer in common ought always be short, and when the sign is given by the superior [abbot], all should rise together."[7]

This calls to mind Jesus' words in Matthew 6:7-8: "When you pray, do not keep on babbling like pagans, for they think they will be heard because of their many words. Do not be like them, for your Father knows what you need before you ask him." The monks' belief that prayer was to be simple and short helped prevent their praying from becoming meaningless periods of gab that went on and on and caused thoughts to drift. Benedict wanted prayer times to be periods of attentiveness and freshness. This was taken seriously, for human frailty was a constant threat to purity in prayer. The monk had to know himself and his weaknesses so as not to abuse the sacred trust of prayer. Columbanus, an Irish monk who ministered in France and Italy during the late sixth and early seventh centuries, gave the following advice: "The authentic tradition concerning prayer is that the possibilities of the man consecrated to this work be fulfilled without his getting tired of it. One must keep in mind his possibilities, as well as his mental powers and physical condition. His limitations must be taken into consideration and his possibilities realized according as the measure or fervor of each one requires."[8] Commenting on the *Rule* of Saint Benedict (20), Hildemar wrote on the same principle that "we ought to remain recollected in prayer only during the time that we can, by God's help, remain free of vain thoughts. As soon as we realize that we are being overcome by temptations, and that we do not find delight in prayer, we should arise and return to reading or the recitation of the Psalter or to work."[9]

For the monk, proper attentiveness was crucial in prayer because virtuous prayer was prayer that was unceasingly holy. Such prayer was focused upon eternity, upon others, upon God's thoughts. In the *Conferences* of Cassian the Egyptian abbot, Isaac, speaking of such purity in prayer, said, "The author of eternity would have us ask nothing ephemeral, nothing paltry, nothing transient. He who neglects these petitions for eternity and prefers to ask for the evanescent, insults the generous majesty of God; meanness in prayer offends the judge instead of propitiating him."[10] Unceasing prayer, then, was not just constant praying; it signified a type of prayer—godly prayer.

The Pastoral Prayer of Abbot Aelred, leader of the Christian abbey of Rievaulx in Northumbria (ca. 1150), is such a prayer. It is oriented upon the eternal. Following is a glimpse (from that writing) into his remarkable life of prayer.[11]

As leader of the monastery, Aelred was awed by the responsibility, humbled by his office. He began by referring to himself as a "wretchful, unfit bungler of a shepherd," contrasting himself with Jesus, "O good shepherd (John 10:11, 14)." He puzzled over why God had placed him in his position as abbot, and before he dared to pray for those under his care, he confessed his sins—a "sacrifice of prayer." Scarred from past sins, guilty of present iniquity and certain of future failures (all of which he knew God saw), he uttered quietly and confidently, "Look well at me, sweet Lord, look well. I place my hope in your compassion." Glancing back at Solomon's prayer in 2 Chronicles 1:10, where David's son prayed not for riches but for wisdom to rule, Aelred pleaded to God for wisdom, saying, "Send her [wisdom] forth, O fount of wisdom, from the throne of your glory that she may . . . order the thoughts and words and all my deeds and counsel."

He told the Lord that he wished to "be holy and utterly employed and expended" for those under his care. Here was a man consumed with his pastoral charge. He then asked to be taught by the Holy Spirit in the following areas: being patient with the frail; sympathizing kindly; supporting tactfully; consoling the sad; strengthening the fainthearted; raising the fallen; being weak with the weak; being indignant with those who have been scandalized; chiding the restless; comforting the timid; sustaining the weak; adapting himself to various temperaments, characters, feelings and degrees of intelligence or simplicity; and speaking words that would build up in faith, hope, love, sexual purity, humility, patience and obedience (compare 1 Cor 9:22; 13:13; 2 Cor 11:29; Eph 4:29).

In the final part of his prayer Aelred asked God to unify those under his charge in peace, to build them up in faith, to strengthen them against temptation and trial, and to free them from vices that would deter them from faithfulness (compare Mt 6:13; Eph 4:3). Near the end of his prayer he said warmly,

"You know, sweet Lord, how much I love them, how my heart goes out to them and melts for them." Here is a shepherd after the Shepherd's own heart, one consumed with the Christian growth of his charges, their life in the Spirit. He closed by petitioning the Lord to "cheer the depressed, fan the lukewarm into flame, and reinforce the wavering."

Another stunning example is Anselm's *Prayer for Enemies*. Besides praying the words of Scripture, he also prayed, as Scripture commanded him to pray, after the words of Jesus, "You have heard that it was said 'Love your neighbor and hate your enemy.' But I tell you: Love your enemies and pray for those who persecute you that you may be sons of your Father in heaven" (Mt 5:43-45). In his prayer for those who had persecuted him we find the prayers of a mature Christian heart: a heart that admitted its tendency to hate in return; a heart that needed the intervention of God to love; a heart that sought eternal blessings for his foes; a heart that recognized its own scandalous nature.

> I can begin nothing good without you,
> neither can I bring anything to fruition
> nor maintain it, without you. . . .
>
> You, who are true light, lighten their darkness;
> You, who are whole truth, correct their errors;
> You, who are true life, give life to their souls. . . .
>
> Tender Lord Jesus,
> let me not be the cause of the death of my brothers,
> let me not be to them
> a stone of stumbling and a rock of offense.
> For it is more than enough, Lord,
> that I should be a scandal to myself
> my sin is sufficient to me.[12]

Here, in Aelred and Anselm, are two examples of maturity and purity in prayer.

Brevity aided such purity. So 1 Thessalonians 5:17 and 1 Timothy 2:8 go together, as Isaac reminds us: "St. Paul's words were: 'Pray without ceasing,' and 'In every place lifting up pure hands without wrath and controversy.' To obey this is impossible, unless the mind is purified from sin, is given to virtue as its natural good, and is continually nourished by the contemplation of God."[13] And once again: "He prays too little, who only prays when he is on his knees. But he never prays, who while on his knees is in his heart roaming far afield."[14]

But besides being brief and therefore attentive and pure, the monks' prayers were to be frequent. Like studying for an exam or memorizing a poem, many short, concentrated periods are better than a few drawn-out, disjointed ones. Though these dedicated men prayed short prayers, they prayed many times each day. Their praying was "without ceasing," that is, frequent. Their day typically would begin about 2:00 a.m. in winter or 3:00 a.m. in the summer. Prayer at the first hour (6:00 a.m.) was followed by prayer at the third, sixth and ninth hours, for which the monks interrupted their labor, and then evening prayer. It was not strange, however, for monks to practice prayer after what they understood as the manner of David (Ps 119:164). This would involve seven periods of prayer, including the middle of the night and before dawn.

Prayer, of course, also accompanied work and meals and the weekly, longer liturgical services. "Pray without ceasing," then, also meant praying continually in all daily involvement. Douglas Burton-Christie relates a wonderful story from the early desert monks:

> This story concerns some Euchites [a heretical sect], who went to see Abba Lucious. When Lucious asked them about their work, they replied, "We do not touch manual work but as the Apostle says, we pray without ceasing (1 Thess 5:17)." Lucious was dubious about this reply and pressed his visitors to elaborate. He asked them whether they ever ate or slept. They replied

that they did. Lucious then asked how they prayed when they were eating or sleeping, but they could not find an answer to give him. Seeing this, he said to them, in language which expressed the depth of their misunderstanding of the biblical text, "Forgive me but you do not act as you speak." Lucious then proceeded to show them how, while doing his manual work, he prayed without ceasing. He told them: "I sit down with God, soaking my reeds and plaiting my ropes and saying to God, 'have mercy on me . . . save me from my sins.' "[15]

Bible Reading and Meditation

Monastic prayer was also united with the reading of the Bible. For many monks it was difficult to separate the two, for prayer was prayerful reading. In this spirit Arnoul of Bohériss wrote, "When he reads, let him seek for savor, not science. The Holy Scripture is the well of Jacob from which the waters are drawn which will be poured out later in prayer. Thus there will be no need to go to the oratory [spoken prayer] to begin to pray; but in reading itself, means will be found for prayer and contemplation."[16]

Reading the Bible encouraged prayer, nurtured sacred thinking, helped the monks think correctly about God and themselves. Fragmenting one's devotional life into separate functions such as Bible study time, meditation and prayer time is largely a modern invention. But monks wed them as different aspects of one act. In his worshipful theological work *Meditation on Human Redemption,* Anselm (1033–1109) wrote:

Consider again the strength of your salvation and where it is found. Meditate upon it, delight in the contemplation of it. Shake off your lethargy and set your mind to thinking over these things. Taste the goodness of your Redeemer, be on fire with love for your Savior. Chew the honeycomb of his words, suck their flavor which is sweeter than sap, swallow their wholesome sweetness. Chew by thinking, suck by understanding, swallow by loving and rejoicing. Be glad to chew, be thankful to suck, rejoice to swallow.[17]

For Anselm, sacred reading "was an action of the whole person, by which the meaning of a text was absorbed, until it became prayer."[18] Reading the Bible in prayer involved what the monks often spoke of as rumination—a meditative, reflective thinking or contemplation. Such reading could be slow, but that was okay. So deep and thorough was the rumination of some monks that they memorized great portions of the Bible. One such monk, the thirteenth-century Antony of Padua, was said to have known almost the entire Bible by heart. This ability caused Gregory IX to refer to him as "the Ark of the Covenant." By that, he meant that much as the ark held the tablets of the law of Moses, Antony retained "the whole of Scripture in his memory."[19]

The Psalms attracted the monks the most, although they weren't hesitant about reading all the Scriptures and even commentaries on them. Through such contemplative reading their prayers ultimately became citations or paraphrases of Scripture, and through memorization unceasing prayer became more possible. Their mouths uttered and their minds presented to God what was in their hearts. It was not enough simply to keep the appointed times of prayer, as Epiphanius, the bishop of Cyprus, relates: "The true monk should have prayer and psalmody continually in his heart."[20] For this reason memorization of the Psalter was a regular requirement of the monastic life.[21] Recitation of the Psalms to aid prayer could reach astounding measures, with a few monks reciting the entire Psalter. Although some degrees of recitation seem severe, it was aimed at uniting the heart, tongue and mind in prayer. The Scripture was the fountain of all practice for the monk, and it supplied every avenue to spirituality. Epiphanius said, "Ignorance of the Scriptures is a precipice and a deep abyss." Antony said every monk should heed this teaching: "Whatever you do, do it according to the testimony of the holy Scriptures."[22] Reading, memorizing and reciting the Scriptures led to purity in prayer, for one prayed after the mind of God as one began to personally own the biblical revelation and to utter it back to God.

Monastic prayer, in its unity with Bible reading, has three phases forming a unified practice.[23] The first phase is *lectio,* or reading. This is a practice devoted to the reading of Holy Scripture or helpful explanations of it from within the church. The focus is upon literature that is sacred, divine in origin, so it is called *lectio divina.* Joined to the first phase is the second term, *meditatio,* or meditation. *How* one reads is critical to both *lectio* and *meditatio.* Seeing the words on the page is not sufficient. One must use the mouth, pronouncing the words, owning them in both mind and body. Thus, when the monks speak of hearing the Scriptures, this is not merely a figure of speech for silent reading. It emphasizes the vocal aspect of monastic reading. It is this vocal recitation, done repetitively, that leads to memorization of the Bible and the beginning of internalization. Note these emphases within early monasticism on the regular repetition of Scripture, leading to memorization and then purity:

> There shall be no one whatever in the monastery who does not learn to read and does not memorize something of the Scriptures. [One should learn by heart] at least the New Testament and the Psalter.[24]

> Let us devote ourselves to reading and learning the Scriptures, reciting them continually, aware of the text, "A man shall be filled with the fruit of his own mouth" (Prov 13:2). . . . Consider by how many testimonies the word of the Lord urges us to recite the Holy Scriptures that we may possess through faith what we have repeated with our mouth.[25]

The final phase is *oratio,* or prayer. It is last because it is founded on the first two. Reading and meditation must lead to response or they are incomplete, inauthentic. Reading and meditation do not exist in and of themselves for the monk;

they serve prayer. *Lectio divina* and *meditatio* are slow, reflective and repetitive. The monks follow Jesus' own pattern of repetition in prayer of the same words (Mt 26:44) as the words of Scripture inform and even become their own prayer. Leclercq helpfully defines monastic prayer from this viewpoint. It is "our placing our voice in harmony with the voice of God in the Church and in ourselves, in harmonizing our voice with his."[26] This happens only as the Bible accompanies prayer.

A premier example of this is in Anselm's *Prayer to Christ,* in which one hears echoes of at least five psalms. Let's steal a glimpse of this Christian leader in humble, tearful prayer.

> Most kind lover of men,
> "the poor commits himself to you,
> for you are the helper of the orphan" [Ps 10:14].
> My most safe helper,
> have mercy upon the orphan left to you.
> I am become a child without a father;
> my soul is like a widow . . . .
> "My soul thirsts for you, my flesh longs after you" [Ps 63:1; 42:2].
> My soul thirsts for God, the fountain of life;
> "when shall I come to appear before the presence
>   of God?" [Ps 42:2].
> My consoler, for whom I wait, when will you come?
> O that I might see the joy that I desire;
> that I might be satisfied with the appearing of your glory
> for which I hunger;
> that I might be satisfied with the riches of your house
> for which I sigh;
> that I might drink of the torrent of your pleasures
> for which I thirst [Ps 36:8].[27]

The language of Scripture had become Anselm's prayer language. He had assimilated God's Word into his very speech; his mind was so saturated with it that he spoke back to God what God had spoken to him.

Intimacy, Doctrine and Godly Awareness

As we draw this discussion of monasticism and prayer to a close, I would like us to see three final aspects of the monks' prayer life.

First, the monks viewed prayer as the treasured occasion of being humbly and gratefully the loved creature before the Creator. Prayer was something desired, something demanding the closing of some doors in order to open the door into prayer. Prayer desperately sought intimacy with God, and prayer began with confession of sin and finiteness and moved into a humble confidence about God's infiniteness and mercy. Note these words by Anselm:

> Come now, little man,
> turn aside for a while from your daily employment,
> escape for a moment from the tumult of your thoughts.
> Put aside your weighty cares,
> let your burdensome distractions wait,
> free yourself awhile for God
> and rest awhile in him.
> [Your servant] longs to see you,
> but your countenance is too far away. . . .
> How wretched is the fate of man
> when he lost that for which he was created. . . .
> Adam [before the Fall] was so full he belched, we are so hungry
> we sigh;
> he had abundance, and we go begging. . . .
>
> Alas, I am indeed wretched,
> one of those wretched sons of Eve,
> separated from God! . . .
> Lord, I am so bent I can only look downwards,
> raise me, that I may look upwards.
> My iniquities have gone over my head,
> they cover me and weigh me down like a heavy burden. . .
>
> Ah, from what generous love and loving generosity
> compassion follows out to us!

> Ah, what feelings of love should we sinners have
> towards the unbounded goodness of God! . . .
> I was seeking God,
> and I have found that he is above all things,
> and that than which nothing greater can be thought.[28]

Second, in Anselm and in many others we see hardly any distinction between a robust theology and devotion, between head and heart, doctrine and practical piety, knowledge and prayer. The prayers of earlier monks were nurtured on and reflected a foundation of definite belief in orthodox doctrines. One who prayed purely did not pray with mere sentimentality. Prayer was not an occasion for informality with the Judge and Creator of the universe. One was obligated to believe correctly about God and his relationship to creation. Such belief, then, was to find expression in theologically correct prayer. Purity in prayer began with believing the theology held and taught by the church. Prayer was an opportunity to enter into a deeper understanding of the church's faith. Two of Anselm's greatest theological treatises, *Meditation on Human Redemption* and *Proslogion,* it is important to note, are prayers. Read with me his tender, profound reflection upon the mysterious death of Christ, the God-man:

> There is something mysterious in this abjection. O hidden strength: a man hangs on a cross and lifts the load of eternal death from the human race; a man nailed to wood looses the bonds of everlasting death that hold fast the world. O hidden power: a man condemned with thieves saves men condemned with devils, a man stretched out on the gibbet draws all men to himself. O mysterious strength: one soul coming forth from torment draws countless souls with him out of hell, a man submits to the death of the body and destroys the death of souls. . . . See, Christian soul, here is the strength of your salvation, here is the cause of your freedom, here is the price of your redemption. You were a bondslave and by this man you are free. By him you are brought back from exile, lost, you are restored, dead, you are raised.[29]

Finally, prayer was an enduring awareness of God. It might await set times for communal or private expression, but it was ultimately a constant discipline of meditation upon one's finitude in light of God's immensity. To aid this enduring awareness, some monks adopted biblical texts that expressed their state in numerous specific instances. Abbot Isaac was one of these. Psalm 70:1—"O God, make speed to save me; O LORD, make haste to help me"—was for him a text that fit "every mood and temper of human nature, every temptation, every circumstance. It contains an invocation of God, a humble confession of faith, a reverent watchfulness, a meditation upon our frailty, a confidence in God's answer, an assurance of his ever-present support. The man who continually invokes God as his guardian, is aware that he is continually at hand."[30] Each believer needed to cling to this passage. When one felt gluttonous, when one was weak about reading the Bible, when a temptation came softly, when anger welled up, when pride crept in, when wandering thoughts interrupted prayer, when one thought stumbling was unlikely, the prayer must be sincerely spoken.[31]

Anselm's biographer, Eadmer, and Anselm himself tell us that his prayers were written to benefit others in their prayer lives. This monk, who was also a theologian, delivered his prayers to help the people enter into transforming conversations with Almighty God. As Eadmer expressed it, "I hope that [the reader's] heart will be touched and that he will feel the benefit of them [the prayers] and rejoice in them and for them."[32]

The Pope, the Church and the Ruler (Part 2)
Early in the thirteenth century the papacy attained a level of authority, efficiency and organization never before known. Pope Gregory VII (1073–1085) claimed papal authority in the temporal, secular arena as well as the spiritual, ecclesiastical

realm. Then papal power reached its height in Pope Innocent III (1198–1216). Innocent III claimed that even kings and nobles derived their authority from the pontiff. Not all rulers recognized or submitted to this view, and the disagreements between some royals and popes make for some of the most intriguing stories in medieval history. And yet the pope, as the supposed descendant of the apostle Peter and as head of the church, received the undying faithfulness of many rulers.

In exercising this authority the church of the Middle Ages became a sophisticated administrative organization. More involvement in civil and political decisions, struggles with rulers, territorial claims, even the development and employment of an army increased the papacy's complex bureaucracy. Such complexity and entanglement with secular, civil and political concerns resulted in a blurring of the church's pilgrim identity and its focus on the Great Commission. The emphasis on ecclesiastical office and clergy resulted in an increased separation between clergy and laity. Theology and spirituality became more and more the exclusive functions of the clergy. In the fourteenth century the papal structure, contrary to the assertions of Pope Boniface VIII in 1301 and 1302, began to lose the prominence over secular rulers it had earlier enjoyed. Kings and nobles became less sensitive to papal edicts, and at times papal methods of control became less than honorable, more in keeping with worldly rather than heavenly pursuits.

The institutional church's orientation toward the earthly can also be seen in its Crusades in the twelfth and thirteenth centuries. The earthly, of course, was the Holy Land, which had been occupied by Muslims for several hundred years. The land of redemptive events and revelation, inhabited by the faithful of Islam, was a stone in the shoes of the papacy, the Christian kings and much of the populace of Western Europe. Promised spiritual reward for reclaiming the land for Christianity was a great motivator for the devout. Others, however, found interest in the promise of adventure and captured wealth. Ultimately the Christian goals failed and distracted the church from its more noble duties. The sword and the lance rarely contributed to anyone's being salt and light.

It was in the Fourth Crusade (1202–1204) that a relationship already characterized by miserable fracture and division received further insult. In 1054 the Western Roman Church, represented by delegates sent by Pope Leo IX, excommunicated the patriarch of Constantinople, the head of the Eastern church. Patriarch Cerularius had refused to acknowledge Rome's supremacy over the Eastern church and, in response to Rome's act, he excommunicated the pope's delegation. This great schism had been anticipated for centuries due to language differences (Latin versus Greek), disagreement over the place of icons in worship, territorial disputes, variant beliefs concerning celibacy and clerical office, and arguments regarding the Holy Spirit's procession (the Eastern church said the Spirit proceeded only from the Father, while the Western church said he proceeded from both the Father and the Son). The dark act of 1204 was the sacking of Constantinople by Western crusaders. Only after the Second Vatican Council (1962–1965) did serious reconciliation between the Western and Eastern churches begin. In 1965 the sentences of excommunication were removed in Jerusalem at a meeting between Pope Paul VI and Patriarch Athenagoras.

Scholasticism

In the midst of the institutional development of the church and its wars, the thirteenth century also gave birth to a particular emphasis in the method of doing theology. Known as Scholasticism, this approach began with the doctrines the church already held as indispensable and sought to explain them by combining reason, faith, Scripture and tradition. The Scholastics—those who engaged in this endeavor—worked hard at thinking through what they already held by faith. They labored to find a meeting place for trust and knowledge, belief and reason. They desired to serve the church by setting a table where faith and understanding dined joyously together.

Ultimately these theologians believed that "Christian theology . . . is not naked faith, but faith invested by grace with reason and imagination."[33] Spirituality, life in the Spirit of God, was not to be viewed as a pious, hopeful wish in something basically irrational and unreasonable. Rather, spirituality involved thinking as much as feeling, pondering as much as sensing, brain work as much as willing, head as much as heart. New doctrine was not their interest. They were not attracted to novelty. Neither did they think they could or should erase all mystery from faith. What they did concentrate on was enlarging the church's mental growth in the faith so that one didn't just say the creed in blind, ambiguous "faith" but appreciated its depths, its implications, its riches. Scholastic theologians attempted to explain the reasonableness of the creed. They explained *why* the church's beliefs made good sense. One shouldn't say "I believe that the Son is one essence with the Father" as if it is nonsense and as if there is a super-spirituality in believing poppycock. Instead, while saying the creed, one should rejoice that the Son is divine, worshiping the Son together with the Father and determining not to confuse the person of the Son with the person of the Father.

Thomas Aquinas, perhaps the greatest medieval Scholastic, said we do not employ reason to test, try or prove faith. Rather, sacred doctrine "uses human reasoning . . . to make manifest some implications of its [faith's] message. . . . Natural reason should assist faith."[34] In other words, reason or rational argumentation is not the authority that ultimately renders a verdict in favor of faith. Rather, reason assists faith by helping us grasp its reasonableness and its significance. But reason never substitutes for revelation or faith. As Anselm said, "Lord I am not trying to make my way to your height, for my understanding is no way equal to that, but I do desire to understand a little of your truth which my heart already believes and loves. I do not seek to understand so that I may believe, but I believe so that I may understand; and what is more, I believe that unless I do believe I shall not understand."[35]

The Scholastic theologians help us recall Jesus' words in Matthew 22:37-38: "Love the Lord your God with all your *heart* and with all your *soul* and with all your *mind*. This is the first and the greatest commandment" (italics added).

Most of us are more familiar with moral virtue than we are with the virtue of the intellect. The Scholastics would all emphasize the importance of qualities such as charity, humility, faithfulness, generosity and self-control. But they believed that other qualities were essential to Christianity as well. These included perception, comprehension, understanding, wisdom, truthfulness and discernment. According to the Scholastics, regenerate, Spirit-indwelt human beings were to engage their minds. Thinking well was integral to being well.[36] They considered the opposites of the intellectual virtues (foolishness, senselessness, delusion, fallaciousness, error, inaccuracy, miscalculation, disorientation, derangement) as dishonorable traits. Because of this they saw the mind as the fount of morality. Paul exhorted the Romans to practice the virtues of humility (in light of spiritual gifts), including love, joy, patience, faithfulness, hospitality, blessing, peace and goodness (Rom 12:3-21). However, before Paul launched into this list of qualities, he gave this command: "Do not conform any longer to the pattern of this world, but be transformed *by the renewing of your mind.* Then you will be able to test and approve what God's will is— his good, pleasing and perfect will" (12:2, italics added). Here is the spirit of the Scholastics.

It is not strange, then, that the rise of the university occurred along with this medieval focus upon intellectual virtues.

Birthed at the end of the twelfth century, medieval universities began as scholars associated with each other and their students. They gathered themselves into educational bodies, groups or universities. Bologna, Paris and Oxford numbered among the most famous early locations.

Mysticism in the Late Middle Ages

In the late Middle Ages (1300–1500) some Christians reacted against the constricting institutionalism of the church and what was perceived as a numbing intellectualism within Scholasticism.[37] These reactions would largely take place on the fringes of institutional church life among ordinary people, who searched hungrily for spiritual vitality, piety and the authenticity of an interior, personal, individual life with God. Spiritual writings in the languages of these hungry souls began to appear, and a great sensitivity to hypocrisy in Christian practice developed.

As the search for the authentic spiritual life outside the institution and intellect gained ground, a mystical orientation to the devotional life emerged. As always happens in reactions, especially those that emphasize the individual and the private to the neglect of the traditional and communal, some of these people were heretical. When you fail to take into account the orthodoxy held by the church in the past and go off on your own, you are prone to wander. But not all these pilgrims in search of spiritual authenticity rebelled against the institution and sought separation from it. Others, more calmly and with reflection, sought rather to restore it to an earlier purity. Where some remained within the institution, seeking to impart renewed meaning and life to traditional practices and symbols, others revolted against what they perceived as vain formalities.

Monks and laypersons alike, in a quest for the soul's transformation, entered into a search for the devotional life. Each hungered for deep personal piety, a more personal encounter with Jesus, spiritual perfection, integrity in repentance and enlightenment and growth through prayer. In many cases there were visions and intense asceticism. Sensations, they believed, also sometimes measured authentic spirituality.

The heretical mystics who ultimately substituted inner experience for outward religious authority viewed themselves as divine, they rejected anything physical or external as unspiritual and they held themselves free from church or moral law. The most popular streams of mysticism, however, emphasized inspirational experiences and feelings that reflected intense, immediate, inner contact with God and found some harmony between the mind and the heart. In many ways the mysticism of the late Middle Ages was an exercise in spirituality, a practice of private reflection and prayer in the shadow of institution and intellect.

Themes common to medieval mystics were detachment from self and the world, selflessness, and the experience of the fullness of God. Mystical souls craved intimacy and fellowship with God. They longed for a temporal taste of the presence of God in their souls, a momentary, experiential awareness of God's presence unobscured by sin and darkness. An ecstatic love for God, usually identified with ecstatic joy, was the destination of the mystics' journey. They wanted to feel themselves as nothing and God as everything.

The Song of Solomon was a favorite text for contemplating the soul's sublime knowledge of God. The mystics viewed the book as presenting a spiritual marriage between the individual soul and God as well as between the church and Christ. These believers wanted to lean on Jesus' breast (Jn 13:23, 25) and to rest under the comforting wings of Jesus, in contrast to stubborn Jerusalem (Lk 13:34). This relationship could also be viewed in terms of the promised abode for the Father and Son within the believer (Jn 14:23). It stood out against the backdrop of the many New Testament passages that speak of the Holy Spirit's presence in the believer's body (1 Cor 3:16; 6:19; see also Rom 5:5). Along with Peter's statement that believers are participants in the divine nature (2 Pet 1:4), these passages encouraged the mystics to seek to experience more fully a union that already existed by grace. They identified with the psalmist's words that "my flesh and heart may fail, but God is . . . my portion forever" (Ps 73:26). Recognizing that, like Paul, each of them was "a wretched man," desperately in need of delivery from the "body of death," the mystics thirsted for a conscious oneness with God.[38]

The writings of some medieval mystics are quite inspirational and instructive. We would be poorer in our devotional literature without them.

Although not a late medieval spiritual author, Bernard of Clairvaux (1090–1153) tuned the strings that others later would play. In his text entitled *On the Love of God* he began with the following statement: "You wish me to tell you why God should be loved, and in what way or measure we should love him. I answer then: the reason for our loving God *is* God; and measure of that love there should be none. . . . God is not loved without reward, although he should be loved without reward in view. True charity [love] is never left with empty hands; and yet she is no hireling, out of pay, but 'seeketh not her own' [1 Cor 13:5]."[39]

Meister Eckhart (1260–1327), a late medieval mystic, wrote in his *On Solitude and the Attainment of God* how we are to think of God. In this writing he emphasized that if time and place control our thoughts of God, if we differentiate between the sacred locations and moments on the one hand and the secular on the other, we have not yet found true union with God. Meditating about God is to be a lifestyle, not an activity.

> One ought to keep hold of God in everything and accustom his mind to retain God always among his feelings, thoughts, and loves. Take care how you think of God. As you think of him in church or closet, think of him everywhere. Take him with you among the crowds and turmoil of the alien world.

You should, however, maintain the same mind, the same trust, and the same earnestness toward God in all your doings. . . . On the other hand, the person who is not conscious of God's presence, but who must always be going out to get him from this and that, who has to seek him by special methods, as by means of some activity, person, or place—such people have not attained God.[40]

The devotional writings of the late Middle Ages were not limited to men. The quest for the spiritual life was, of course, a woman's journey as well. And the women mystics, prominent in the thirteenth century, have left us an important body of literature. Mysticism for them was "an alternative to the authority of office," that is, office that was exclusively male and clerical, denied to women and laity.[41] Yet it complemented the clerical office rather than challenged it. The women's visions affirmed the priests and at the same time offered women and laity a mode of spirituality that was ambivalent about power and authority.[42]

One theological emphasis to emerge was that of God's accessibility and comprehensibility. The women mystics desired to show God as loving and approachable and turned to analogies of human relationships to assist them in that endeavor. The theme of God's accessibility was poignantly captured for them in the reality that "Christ is what we are" in the miracle of incarnation that joined divinity to humanity.[43] The image they offered was Jesus as mother. Flowering first in the twelfth century out of biblical metaphors (Is 66:13; Mt 23:37), the maternal imagery described Jesus' tender, nurturing, consoling virtues in human terms that, although helpful, did not exhaust his immensity. Julian of Norwich, who died in 1413, was an English mystic whose *Book of Showings* is a description of spiritual lessons on love for God. She provides an indispensable glimpse into the analogy:[44]

Jesus Christ who does good against evil is our true Mother—we have our being from Him where the basis of motherhood begins, with all the sweet protection of love that accompanies it endlessly.

All the fair action and all the sweet natural function of dearworthy motherhood is attached to the Second Person; for in Him we have this divine will whole and safe without end, both in nature and grace, from His own excellent goodness.

In the following selection she teaches us that true rest and solace are found only in the Creator:

This is the reason why we are not fully at ease in heart and soul: because here we seek rest in these things that are so little, in which there is no rest, and we recognize not our God who is all powerful, all wise, all good, for He is the true rest.

God wishes to be known, and He delights that we remain in Him, because all that is less than He is not enough for us.

And this is the reason why no soul is at rest until it is emptied of everything that is created. When the soul is willingly emptied for love in order to have Him who is all, then is it able to receive spiritual rest.[45]

The mystics craved what Eugene H. Peterson calls transcendence, which is essential to human fullness. *"Transcendence:* we want to experience divine love and trust and joy. We are not ourselves by ourselves. . . . We hunger for divine meaning, someone who will touch us. . . . We hunger for communion with God, something beyond the satisfaction of self, the development of *me.* We are fed up with being told *about* God."[46]

Peterson says that, along with transcendence, another essential to Christian spirituality is what he calls intimacy—an experience of being loved by humans and having trust and joy in those relationships. Spirituality takes into account both love of God and love of neighbor. The mystics emphasized the first, though most also saw the second as a necessary complement. Peterson, in his contemporary paraphrase of some psalms, helps to capture the heart of the mystical spirit of the latter period of the Middle Ages:

A white-tailed deer drinks
    from the creek;
I want to drink God,
    deep draughts of God.
I'm thirsty for God-alive.
I wonder, "Will I ever make it—
    arrive and drink in God's presence?" (Ps 42:1-2, The Message)

God—you're my God!
    I can't get enough of you!
I've worked up such hunger and thirst for God,
    traveling across dry and weary desert. (63:1, The Message)

You're all I want in heaven!
    You're all I want on earth!
When my skin sags and my bones get brittle,
    Yahweh is rock-firm and faithful.
Look! Those who left you are falling apart!
    Deserters, they'll never be heard from again.
But I'm in the very presence of God—
    oh, how refreshing it is!
I've made Lord Yahweh my home.
    God, I'm telling the world what you do! (73:25-28, The Message)

The medieval period was rich with Christian life: the eager search for intimacy with the living God as well as constant prayer and careful thinking in edifying relationships with other believers. At the same time, though, there was an encroaching poverty: the institutionalization of the spiritual community that plundered freedom, laity and simplicity. From monastic reforms to lay preachers to female spirituality to devotionalism and mysticism, Christians separated themselves from that impoverishment in search of the wealth of life in the Spirit. We have barely scratched the surface of that journey's history. As our study continues, we will investigate the church in the age of reform during the third part of our survey.

Part 3

Gold Sovereigns
The Church in the Protestant Reformation

In ancient Europe and North Africa many houses of the rich had floors made out of artistically placed small tiles of various colors. These mosaic tiles were cemented into the floor to render a design or a picture of some sort—a scene of wild animals, fish or geometrical shapes. The stones had to be positioned carefully. If you rearranged them, some other design would be produced or there would be some disarray with no design at all. This is what the Reformers felt happened at the end of the Middle Ages: the pieces of the true doctrines of salvation, church and Scripture got mixed up and needed to be sorted out.

Or we could look at church doctrine as a jewel-filled crown in which the Reformers thought some priceless jewels had been replaced by counterfeits and the gold had become tarnished. They needed to shine the gold and authenticate the jewels. Many of the themes we have seen before will appear again.

5

A River with Many Tributaries

FLOWING SOME THIRTY-NINE HUNDRED MILES from west to east, the Amazon River is the world's second longest river. The Nile River takes first place in that category. Yet the Amazon's drainage basin is the world's largest. Several tributaries of varying sizes and colors nurture it. With its origin in the Aporimac and Maranon rivers, both of which are fed by cold streams of the Andes Mountains, the Amazon proceeds eastward to the Atlantic Ocean. On its way the yellowish Madeira, the blackish Rio Negro and the emerald-greenish Tapajos feed it. Each contributes to the river's power and grandeur, so that its output, near the Atlantic Ocean, is over 7.5 million cubic feet of water per second. This output constitutes the greatest river discharge in the world.

The Reformation, too, gained its character and success from many sources. Though at its center a theological movement, it was nurtured through a complex of important factors. And although something new, it also echoed themes and concerns that were old.

Mysticism

Along with the medieval mystics and the Renaissance (in the fourteenth through the sixteenth centuries), the Reformation shared a disenchantment about elements within the later Middle Ages. That era was seen largely as an era of corruption within the clergy—corruption in which formalism, superstition and institution had replaced authenticity in spirituality. Furthermore, some believed that Scholasticism had majored on unessential, obscure speculation rather than basic issues of faith. Such evaluations were overdone, as we saw in the previous chapter. But the Christian humanists of the Renaissance, the mystics and the Reformers did have some worthwhile bones to pick with their contemporaries and the earlier centuries. In some of their complaints the Reformers were echoing earlier disillusionment and attempts at reform.[1]

As noted earlier, the mysticism of the Middle Ages was a quest for a deeper, more authentic devotional life. In part it was fueled by disappointments with clerical leadership. Many believers had grown skeptical about the clergy's morality and its qualifications for leading people into spirituality. Along with the believers' reservations about the clergy came similar skepticism about whether the public, social arena was the true location for spirituality. The church as an institution made public ritual the prevailing view of the spiritual life. In reaction to these questions about the adequacy of the clergy and the liturgy, some believers responded by withdrawing from the public arena and concentrating instead on inner reflection, morality and a simple life. To a degree, elements of the Reformation continued the impulse of these mystics toward simplicity rather than ritual, toward private reflection rather than public liturgy and toward inner contemplation rather than outward, institutional form.

Christian Humanism

In addition to mysticism, the Protestant Reformation had a

second tributary: the Christian humanism of the Renaissance. The term *humanism* is related to the humanities—the arts and sciences, particularly literature, painting, sculpture, architecture, music. The Christian humanists focused on returning to the sources, the classics, and to the way things were before the extravagance and complexity of the Middle Ages. They were convinced that the primitive simplicity and integrity of Christianity had been buried under layers of public religion, clerical control and institutionalization of the church. Authentic Christianity was like the sweet, tangy, juicy sections of an orange—before you could enjoy the fruit, you had to peel the skin and dispense with the rind.

A representative Christian humanist was Desiderius Erasmus (1469–1536). Two aspects of his work captured the interests of humanism. First, in a time when the Vulgate—Jerome's Latin translation of the Scriptures—was the Bible of the day, Erasmus produced a reliable Greek text of the New Testament. Erasmus's recovery of the Greek reveals the humanist quest for a return to primitive spirituality. He felt that the original Greek of the New Testament, not a translation, offered the best hope for a recovery of authentic Christianity. It was the sharpest knife to deal with the skin and rind.

Second, in a time when externals—public liturgy and the hierarchy of clergy and institution—were emphasized, Erasmus stressed another avenue to spirituality. For him, spirituality was also a matter for the individual layperson, and it centered around obedience to Christ's teachings. Inner conviction rather than ritualistic formalism fueled such obedience. Spirituality was first a matter of *inner* conversion, an attitude of heart and mind. Visible externals were rubbish without the invisible internal reality.

In 1501 Erasmus wrote a tract entitled *The Handbook of the Christian Soldier* on Christian morals and spirituality. It cuts to the heart of Christianity, stressing the authentic inner life. Join me in a trip behind the woodshed where Erasmus helps build our character through ancient words written to believers of the Middle Ages who struggled within a world of visible, external formalism.

> The body may be covered with a monk's cowl, but what good is that if the mind wears a worldly garb?
>
> In a visible place of worship you kneel on bodily knees; but nothing is accomplished thereby if in the shrine of the heart you stand erect in defiance of God.
>
> You venerate the wood of the cross; better to follow the mystery of the cross.
>
> You observe fasts and abstain from things that do not defile a man, and you do not refrain from obscene speech which defiles both your own and the author's conscience.
>
> The body does not commit adultery, but by your cupidity your mind is adulterous.
>
> You hear the word of God with your bodily ears; listen rather within.
>
> You confess your sins to a priest, who is a mere man; take care how you confess them to God. For to confess them inwardly to him is to have hatred for them. . . . I am not concerned with what you manifest externally. . . . I prefer that you hate your vicious habits once for all, truly and from within, than that you detest them ten times verbally before a priest.[2]

Erasmus's emphasis on the inner person came through in his reflection on the nature of God. Jesus said to the Samaritan woman in John 4:24 that "God is spirit, and his worshipers must worship in spirit and truth." Erasmus quoted an ancient Roman poet to make the point that even some pagans were aware of this fact about the divine nature and of the need to worship in purity of mind. He wrote that external, bodily "works are not condemned, but those that are invisible are preferred. Visible worship is not condemned, but God is appeased only by invisible piety."[3] For biblical support he mentioned Psalm 51:16-17:

> You do not delight in sacrifice, or I would bring it;
>> you do not take pleasure in burnt offerings.
> The sacrifices of God are a broken spirit;
>> a broken and contrite heart,
>> O God, you will not despise.

Erasmus's highlighting of the interior aspect of spirituality in a culture controlled by external ritual was one of his avenues to authentic Christianity. Another aspect, as mentioned briefly, was his quest to return to the primary source of theology: the Scriptures in their original languages. Reading the Bible in Greek or Hebrew, he said, does not automatically give a person mastery of God's message. He did believe, however, that undue dependence on translations keeps people that much further from a true understanding of the Bible.[4] Studying the Scriptures in the original languages, he taught, could aid our insight.

Erasmus was fighting a naive assumption that contemporary translations and contemporary commentators were void of error. He pleaded for Christians to go back to the Greek in order to hear the gospel directly from God. The Bible was to be sung by the farmer as he plowed and the weaver as she operated the shuttle; it was not meant to be limited to the hands of the priest.[5] But the theologian or Christian leader who taught the farmer and weaver what to sing needed to be learning ultimately from the Scriptures, not from the infatuations of that age or a past age.[6] Thus Erasmus encouraged a return to the original languages as a means of guarding against being controlled by interpretations that might lead astray. He brought into the sixteenth century what the Bereans practiced in the first century, the testing of interpretations of the Bible against the Bible: "Now the Bereans were of more noble character than the Thessalonians, for they received the message [of Paul and Silas] with great eagerness and *examined the Scriptures* every day to see if what Paul said was true" (Acts 17:11, italics added).

The impact of Erasmus's love for the languages, which resulted in his own edition of the Greek New Testament, can be seen in its effect on the reformer Ulrich Zwingli (1484–1531).[7] Securing a copy of Erasmus's 1516 edition of the New Testament, Zwingli found himself captivated by the original text. Overcome by the epistles of Paul, he copied them by hand in Greek and committed them to memory. He freshly and zealously gave himself to Christ and to the gospel ministry.

Scholasticism

Besides mysticism and humanism, a third tributary into the white-water river of the Protestant Reformation was Scholasticism.[8] While the Reformers adapted the humanists' emphasis on the inner life and the original text of the New Testament, they differed with the humanists on one point. Humanists often judged an idea by its apparent usefulness. An idea or doctrine was true if its practicality to contemporary life was grasped. The ethical consequence of a doctrine determined that doctrine's worth. Pragmatism judged truth: if it works, it's right; if it produces, it's good; if it's practical, it's worthy. The Reformers, however, distanced themselves from this view and returned to the conviction of the Scholastics: an idea, if true, is important for truth's sake. Because God is true, truth as truth matters. The immediate "practicality" or "relevance" of an idea may escape us. Whether it appears pragmatic or not, a true doctrine is to be confessed and upheld.

Erasmus, for one, was willing to reject Luther's view of the bondage of the will merely on the grounds that he thought the doctrine was ethically useless.[9] Even if it was true, he believed, it should not be published. To teach an enslavement to evil was to encourage laziness and godlessness, for people would then sleepily accept their unchangeable plight. But Luther, following in the footsteps of the Scholastics, maintained that ultimate, authentic ethics stem from doctrines that may at first glance seem impractical. As Steven Ozment has said, "For Luther, if a doctrine was true, life had to adjust to it, regardless of the difficulty or the cost; the eternal truth of an idea was more important than its short-term temporal consequences."[10]

The Protestant Reformers, then, both inherited and reacted against elements of mysticism, humanism and Scholasticism. But they also walked in the footsteps of other critics.[11] The Reformers were new, but they were also old. Earlier, in the fourteenth and fifteenth century, John Wycliffe (1330–1384) and John Huss (1372–1415) had addressed issues with which the sixteenth-century Protestant Reformers were sympathetic. Wycliffe and Huss reacted to a church in which the morally bankrupt papacy had become divided between two popes. Rivals of each other, one pope ruled from Rome, the other from Avignon, France. The schism, which began in 1378, was not healed until 1417.

Wycliffe, a professor of theology at Oxford University, raised several issues in reaction. First was the role and nature of the Bible as the sole source of theological authority. It was to be read literally and in the native language of the reader. Second was the nature of the church. The New Testament church was a timeless model to be replicated in every age. And leaders of the church held authority depending on their moral conduct. Third was the role of secular rulers in governing the church. The state, for Wycliffe, should be allowed to judge and punish immoral popes and other members of the clergy. Not received well by university, church or state, Wycliffe was banned from Oxford, dying in obscurity in 1384.

The fate of John Huss, a professor of theology at Prague University, was different. Huss joined Wycliffe in rejecting the authority of an immoral member of the clergy and in stressing the need for clerical piety and virtue. Drawing on some of Wycliffe's writings, he pressed the argument that the king has the authority to supervise the church and its leaders. Yet he went beyond this in *On the Church* (1412) to argue that preachers may preach without the consent of the pope or his bishops. Huss ultimately denied the legitimacy of the high church offices. He became a political liability and was convicted and executed in 1415. One common feature with the successful Protestant Reformation is briefly seen in Wycliffe and Huss: the challenge to the authority of the church's hierarchy.

The Doctrine of Salvation in Peril

A fourth tributary to the Protestant Reformation was the rise of a view of salvation that the Reformers found entirely unacceptable. Though not held by everyone, this view became popular and troublesome. A brief historical review of the doctrine of salvation will help put things in perspective.[12]

Augustine, bishop of Hippo in North Africa (354–430), had taught that although humankind had been created innocent, the Fall changed all that. Since the Fall, humanity has been in bondage to sin and has no freedom from either committing sin or from experiencing its penalties, ultimately including death. The monk Pelagius (350–ca. 425), whose teachings were influential during the first twenty years of the fifteenth century, strongly opposed Augustine's views. For Pelagius, humans were able to choose their own destiny because they had free will and were not chained to inevitable sin. On their own they could choose God and good. Augustine denied such capability, declaring that only God could bring a captive sinner to himself. Another theologian, Duns Scotus (1256–1308), sided more with Augustine and emphasized the importance of God's will over human will.

According to Augustine, God decreed the salvation of a human. A person was saved because God decided to save him or her. A turn back toward Pelagius took place with William of

Ockham (1280–1349) and his followers, the Ockhamists. In their effort to preserve human freedom they weakened the need for God to sovereignly draw fallen humans to himself by a special act of grace. They thought that if God had to cause a person to come to him, that person didn't come to God or love him freely. Like Pelagius, they didn't think that the Fall had damaged a person's ability for moral efforts that would please God. So Ockham, along with Gabriel Biel (1420–1495), taught that the road to salvation began with an individual's efforts produced without the aid of grace from God. God would give grace only as a reward for naturally produced moral effort.

This was the doctrine against which Luther reacted so furiously. For Luther it was vain to think that fallen humanity could contribute anything—even choice—to its own salvation. That's how firmly shackled to sin we are. The words of Luther are clear: "As a matter of fact, without the grace of God the will produces an act that is perverse and evil. On the part of man, however, nothing precedes grace except indisposition and even rebellion against grace. In brief, man by nature has neither correct precept nor good will."[13]

All the tributaries feeding into the river of the Protestant Reformation highlight issues of concern to the Reformers. The Reformation came forth in two streams: Lutheran (in Germany, led by Luther) and Reformed (in Switzerland, led by John Calvin). In the next two chapters we will examine three Reformation issues—salvation, the church and the Scriptures—in an effort to glean insight for our own day.

6

The Doctrine of Salvation in the Reformers

THE FOURTH TRIBUTARY TO THE REFORMATION, Christian soteriology in peril, elicited grave concern and brought forth monumental theological treatises. The Reformers joined the long history of Christians attempting to understand and articulate the pivotal issues of sin, grace, faith, predestination, justification and sanctification. Among these church leaders was Martin Luther.

Luther on Salvation

In September 1517 Luther reacted against the teachings of William of Ockham with the following statements in his *Disputation Against Scholastic Theology:* "It is therefore true that man, being a bad tree, can only will and do evil. . . . We do not become righteous by doing righteous deeds, but having been made righteous, we do righteous deeds."[1]

In October of the same year Luther wrote and distributed his *Ninety-five Theses,* in which, for one thing, he opposed the sale of indulgences. This practice, authorized by papal authority in 1411, had begun in the eleventh century with the teaching that pious service, say, in the Crusades would reduce one's stay in purgatory. In the fifteenth century, guarantees of shorter stays in purgatory in exchange for monies became a regular component of fundraising techniques for the papacy. Objected to by John Huss a century earlier, the sale of indulgences met its master in Luther. His *Theses* were published (probably without his consent) and found immediate popularity among the masses. In the *Theses* Luther attacked the sale of indulgences because they (a) diminished the *free*, gracious gift of salvation; (b) did not evoke true inner contrition or repentance; (c) did not produce the Christian virtue of love, which was true repentance lived outwardly; and (d) were ultimately the opposite of the Christian virtues of mercy and compassion. For Luther, Christianity was about receiving a free gift through a contrite heart, which then distributed love to other needy souls.

Here are a few lines from that historic document: "Any truly repentant Christian has a right to full remission of penalty and guilt, even without indulgence letters [proof of purchase]" *(Thesis* 36). "Any true Christian, whether living or dead, participates in all the blessings of Christ and the church; and this is granted him by God, even without indulgence letters" *(Thesis* 37). "Christians are to be taught that he who sees a needy man and passes him by, yet gives money for indulgences, does not buy papal indulgences but God's wrath" *(Thesis* 45).[2]

We can already taste some of Luther's central themes in these two early writings. Yet, what was the heart of Luther's doctrine of salvation? What concept was dominant in his thinking and in his own conversion? It was the *righteousness of God*. When or how Luther's "breakthrough," his "tower experience," occurred is difficult to say. But clearly it resulted from the coming together of many things: his own reading of the psalms, Paul's epistles and Augustine's writings; his disenchantment with William of Ockham's view, indulgences and the corruption of pope and clergy; and the helpful insights of some contemporaries.

One of those contemporaries was the Roman Catholic Augustinian monk and scholar Johannes von Staupitz (1460–1524). From Staupitz, Luther testified, "the light of the Gospel first began to shine out of the darkness of the heart."[3] Staupitz, whom he called a "messenger from heaven," showed him that the Greek word *metanoia,* which in the Latin translations of the day was rendered "penitence" (that is, "an act of penance"), actually means something else. *Metanoia* is better translated "repentance," and Staupitz taught Luther that at the root of repentance is a "love for justice and God," not some acts or works.[4] Luther then took this seed of thought, fertilized it, watered it and nurtured it until it blossomed into a joyous concept.

Repentance, for Luther, was a "change in one's disposition and [the object of one's] love," a "transformation of one's mind and disposition" through "the grace of God."[5] Repentance was not something a depraved human being had to cook up within himself or herself. It was something God *gave,* something God *did.* The new, transformed disposition was God's new creation. Here is Erasmus's emphasis on the Christian's inside, the pure interior of the converted one.

This "new" insight into repentance as a change that God brings about, and not as the works of humans, was revolutionary. It opened for Luther, a man plagued with the fear of God's righteous wrath against sin, the floodgate of God's gracious provision. Before, Luther understood the phrase "the righteousness of God" to mean "the righteous wrath of God toward evil humanity." But profiting from his insight into repentance, the phrase now came to mean not the righteousness with which God punishes but the righteousness that God gives to sinful humans.

At first, meditating on Romans 1:17, Luther was unable to see how the gospel (the good news of salvation) could be *good* news and yet reveal God's righteousness (understood as wrath). And when meditating on Psalm 31:1, he was confused about how God's righteousness (again, as wrath) could *deliver*. But then he understood. It's best to hear his own words from the preface to the Wittenberg edition of his Latin works:

> As a monk I led an irreproachable life. Nevertheless I felt that I was a sinner before God. My conscience was restless, and I could not depend on God being propitiated by my satisfaction. Not only did I not love, but I actually hated the righteous God who punishes sinners.... Thus a furious battle raged within my perplexed conscience, but meanwhile I was knocking at the door of this particular Pauline passage, earnestly seeking to know the mind of the great Apostle.
>
> Day and night I tried to meditate upon the significance of these words: "The righteousness of God is revealed in it, as written: The righteous shall live by faith." Then, finally, God had mercy on me, and I began to understand that the righteousness of God is that gift of God by which a righteous man lives, namely, faith, and that this sentence—The righteousness of God is revealed in the Gospel—is passive, indicating that the merciful God justifies us by faith, as it is written: 'The righteous shall live by faith.' Now I felt as though I had been reborn altogether and had entered Paradise.[6]

In the spirit of this breakthrough Luther produced many works. We will mention only four here: a sermon and three tractates. The sermon, preached in late 1518 or early 1519, is entitled "Two Kinds of Righteousness" and explains how we enter into a relationship with righteousness. The first treatise, *To the Christian Nobility of the German Nation* (June 1520), exhorted the secular authorities to institute a program of church reform. Later that summer he wrote *The Babylonian Captivity of the Church,* which set forth his view of the sacraments against the controlling customs of the Roman Church. The third treatise, *On the Freedom of a Christian* (November 1520), was a careful explanation of the doctrine of justification and its relationship to the Christian life.

Two of these works, the sermon and the last treatise, are helpful for our understanding of Luther's view of salvation. And they played a role in his later being excommunicated from the Church of Rome. At Leipzig in the summer of 1519 he had already debated some of his views with John Eck, a Roman Catholic scholar. On June 15, 1520, the papal bull *Exsurge Domine* ("Arise, O Lord") was issued, condemning many aspects of Luther's theology and ordering him to retract. Given opportunity and challenged to do so at an assembly of rulers in Worms in the spring of 1521, Luther refused to drift from his convictions based on his interpretation of Scripture and his conscience. In May he was declared an outlaw. Then in 1522 the Reformation really began as German society was swept up in the spirit of reform.

Some of the charges against Luther concerned his teachings on sin and righteousness, both crucial to his views on salvation. We touched earlier on his view of God's righteousness. Now let's go a bit further, using the sermon and treatise mentioned above. In his sermon "Two Kinds of Righteousness," Luther explained that any righteousness coming forth from believers has its source in the righteousness given to them in Christ. There is no intrinsic, human righteousness unless one has first received an "alien," external righteousness from God through Christ. The first type of righteousness (alien) comes, through faith in Christ, as a gift to humans who have no righteousness in themselves but are plagued with evil. This first type then brings forth the second type, which is love of God and neighbor through good works. Imagine Luther's joy at penning such words as these: "Through faith in Christ, therefore, Christ's righteousness becomes our righteousness and all that he has becomes ours; rather he himself becomes ours."[7] Yet joy was joined to challenge: "The second kind of righteousness is our proper righteousness, not because we alone work it, but because we work with that first and alien righteousness. This is that manner of life spent profitably in good works . . . slaying the flesh . . . love to one's neighbor . . . in meekness and fear toward God."[8] Any righteous thought, attitude or action that issues forth from or within an individual has its fountainhead not in his or her depraved humanity but in the righteousness of Christ bestowed on that individual.

In a time when society was emphasizing that salvation as a pathway begins with one's own ability and continues in the structured traditions of the institution of the church, Luther spoke of a salvation separate from our world and ourselves. Salvation comes from outside of us, as does anything we do that is righteous. This righteousness comes from outside ourselves, graciously given by the Father through the Son. Because we are saved by a righteousness that is not ours, Luther affirmed, "the Christian man is both righteous and a sinner, holy and profane, an enemy of God and yet a child of God."[9]

Luther's later work *Freedom of a Christian* begins with a deep, sincere awe and reverence for the virtue of faith. Of faith, the Reformer wrote that "he who has had even a faint taste of it can never write, speak, meditate, or hear enough concerning about it. It is a living 'spring of water welling up to eternal life,' as Christ calls it in John 4."[10] This refreshing, life-giving gift was for Luther the principle that established an apparent contradiction in the Christian's life: "A Christian is perfectly free, lord of all, subject to none" and yet "a Christian is a perfectly dutiful servant of all, subject to all."[11]

Calvin on Salvation

John Calvin's emphasis was similar to Luther's, although Calvin was only twelve when Luther was excommunicated in

1521. Calvin, too, had become severely disenchanted with the Roman Church leadership. He believed that the clergy were misleading and uncaring, and he believed that he himself needed to be redeemed. We are unsure of the precise date of his conversion, but we know that it occurred suddenly sometime between 1532 and 1534. Thereafter he pledged "to dwell at greater length on topics on which the salvation of my hearers depended. For the oracle could never deceive which declares (John 17:3), 'This is eternal life, to know thee the only true God, and Jesus Christ, whom thou has sent.' "[12]

Calvin was trained in law and had a desire to study the classics. But then, changing his interest to theology, Calvin wrote the first edition of his doctrinal masterpiece, *Institutes of the Christian Religion,* in French in 1536 at the age of twenty-seven. Latin editions appeared in 1539, 1543, 1550 and 1559. The same year of the first edition of the *Institutes,* Calvin was encouraged to move to Geneva, where the Reformation was already under way. What Luther had done for the Protestant cause in Germany, Calvin did for that same cause in Switzerland. His first period in Geneva ended in 1538, when the city's government evicted him. In the eyes of the local magistrates he and Guillaume Farel (1489–1565), the leader of the Reformation in Geneva, had placed too much authority in the church and not enough in the city council. Calvin wanted to bring moral and doctrinal reform to the city, but in his plan he left out the council. To Geneva, this brought back memories of life under the Roman bishop before the Reformation.

Calvin left Geneva for Strasbourg, where he remained until he returned, by invitation, to Geneva in September 1541. This time, authority for religious issues lay in the hands of both the church and the city council. He continued to minister in Geneva until his death on May 27, 1564.

Calvin presented the Reformation's classic expression of the doctrine of justification by faith. Just as a person is justified in a court of law before a fair judge if he or she is innocent, so a person would be justified before God by works *if* he or she had works of such purity that God would testify that they were righteous. But since this is impossible, justification is available only through faith: "On the contrary, justified by faith is he who, excluded from the righteousness of works, grasps the righteousness of Christ through faith, and clothed in it, appears in God's sight not as a sinner but as a righteous man. Therefore, we explain justification simply as the acceptance with which God receives us into his favor as righteous men. And we say that it consists in the remission of sins and the imputation of Christ's righteousness."[13]

Calvin's deep conviction about humanity's depravity led him to affirm that even justified believers can never do any righteous deeds on their own. Even regenerated Christians can never offer their works to God as a basis for justification. They are always dependent on Christ's righteousness, because even the "good works" of the godly, when examined in detail, are seen to deserve condemnation.

How, then, did Calvin view good works in the Christian? What is their relationship to salvation? They are to be regarded, he said, "solely as gifts of God," gifts that confirm God's goodness and our calling to salvation.[14] Good works depend on the righteousness given us in Christ, but they do not diminish or supplement it. He quoted Augustine, who said, "See in me thy work, not mine. For if thou seest mine, thou wilt condemn it. If thou seest thine own, thou wilt crown it. For whatever good works are mine are from thee."[15]

Calvin's thinking about salvation and good works was similar to, and yet different from, Luther's. Both Reformers emphasized our desperate need for righteousness outside of ourselves, a righteousness from God—that is, Christ's righteousness by faith. Both stressed that the root of all Christian good works is the righteousness of Christ imparted to us. But they differed on how works relate to the believer. For Luther, Christians are to be devoted to acts and attitudes of righteousness in love for their neighbors. But works could never be the ground of one's sense of security in salvation. Only *faith* was that ground. For Calvin, good works were more firmly a part of the ground of the assurance of salvation.

The Doctrines
of the Church &
the Scriptures
in the Reformers

ANOTHER MAJOR ISSUE IN THE REFORMATION was the doctrine of the church. The question with which the Reformers struggled could be phrased this way: if the church in the late Middle Ages wasn't the hierarchical institution of Rome with its disappointing clergy, what was the church?

The Reformers' common answer put the emphasis on believers. The church was the community of those who truly believed and had been justified by faith. It consisted of those who were "saints" or "holy" in the sense that they had received God's righteousness by faith. This concept was not new—Augustine had taught this—but the institution had all but buried it. Augustine had emphasized that since the true church is invisible, it is ultimately unknowable until the end times. He had found this viewpoint in the parable of the wheat and the weeds (Mt 13:24-30, 36-43).

The Church: Visible and Invisible

The Reformers brushed the dust off this ancient way of thinking and sought to distance themselves from the idea that the church is a visible institution with structures and offices. God's righteousness, which clothes all believers, is invisible. Therefore the church's essence can't be seen. This teaching, however, raised problems. If the church is invisible, unknown until the return of Christ, how should Christians participate in what we call "church"? How could a community of Christians be formed to practice mutual edification and worship?

The wrong answer is to let the idea of community evaporate until Christianity becomes nothing more than individualism. One might think then that if the church is not an institution, if it is not visible and knowable, then Christianity boils down to private experience.

The Reformers wanted to bring change within the whole community of believers, not just individuals. But this caused them to describe visible aspects of the church. In 1539 Luther wrote a treatise entitled *On the Councils and the Church,* in which he presented seven marks or signals that distinguish the true church.

First, the holy Christian people are recognized by their possession of the holy word of God. . . . Now wherever you hear and see this word preached, believed, professed, and lived, do not doubt that the true *ecclesia sancta catholica,* "a Christian holy people," must be there, even though their number is very small.

Second, God's people or the Christian holy people are recognized by the holy sacrament of baptism, wherever it is taught, believed, and administered correctly according to Christ's ordinance.

Third, God's people, or the Christian holy people, are recognized by the holy sacrament of the altar [the Lord's Supper], wherever it is rightly administered, believed, and received, according to Christ's institution.

> Fourth, God's people or holy Christians are recognized exter-
> nally by the office of the keys exercised publicly.[1]

This fourth one needs a bit of explaining. According to
Luther, the "office of the keys" is the church's responsibility to
reprove a believer's sin and seek that Christian's restoration
into fellowship. Church discipline, carried out in the manner
of Matthew 18:15-20, was Luther's concern. His choice of the
term *keys* comes from Jesus' teaching on the keys that bind or
loose on earth what is also bound or loosed in heaven (Mt
16:19). This statement about binding and loosing also occurs in
Matthew 18:18 in the passage on discipline. Luther said that,
seen together, the keys in these two passages are church
reproof and restoration or discipline.

> Fifth, the Church is recognized externally by the fact that it con-
> secrates or calls ministers, or has offices that it is to administer.
> There must be bishops, pastors, or preachers, who publicly and
> privately give, administer, and use the aforementioned four
> things . . . in the name of the Church.
>
> Sixth, the holy Christian people are externally recognized by
> prayer, public praise, and thanksgiving to God.
>
> Seventh, the holy Christian people are externally recognized by
> the holy possession of the sacred cross. They must endure every
> misfortune and persecution, all kinds of trials and evil from the
> devil, the world, and the flesh (as the Lord's prayer indicates) by
> inward sadness, timidity, fear, outward poverty, contempt, ill-
> ness, and weakness, in order to become like their head, Christ.[2]

Luther had this particular biblical text in mind for the last
one: "Blessed are you when people insult you, persecute you
and falsely say all kinds of evil against you because of me.
Rejoice and be glad because great is your reward in heaven, for
in the same way they persecuted the prophets who were before
you" (Mt 5:11-12).

Luther's view of the church, summarized above, was widely

accepted. However, one should not think that the Reformation brought unity to the questions of ecclesiology. For example, Protestants would experience violent division on the issue of baptism. The Anabaptists, who appeared first as the Swiss Brethren in Zurich in 1525, denounced infant baptism and practiced only a baptism of those who were conscious of repentance and faith. The movement found expression in several groups throughout the continent of Europe. Anabaptist beliefs were held and practiced not only by the Swiss Brethren, founded by Conrad Grebel (ca. 1498–1526) and Felix Manz (ca. 1498–1527), but also by the Hutterites of Moravia, led originally by Jacob Hutter (d. 1536), and the Mennonites of Holland (and the surrounding territories), organized by Menno Simons (1498–1561). Joining their teaching on believer's baptism to convictions about nonviolence and nonresistance led the Anabaptists to a refusal to take oaths, to pacifism, to an avoidance of public office and to the rejection of institutional church structures. In consequence, Anabaptists experienced deadly persecution from both Roman Catholics and Protestants. Their view of baptism was seen as especially problematic because it appeared to destroy the foundation of Christian identity. Infant baptism was the rite that served to include the child in the community of grace, faith and salvation. Denial of it was perceived as a denial of Christianity and of Christian society. Felix Manz was drowned on January 5, 1527, in Zurich and thereby became the first Anabaptist martyr. Thousands would follow.

Submission to the Scriptures Leads to Christ

As noted above, Luther stated that the first mark of a church is the possession of the Word of God. But what exactly was the Reformers' view of the Bible? We saw earlier, as well, that Erasmus, as a Christian humanist, championed a return to the original text of the New Testament. His was a quest for the Scriptures unadorned by previous controlling interpretations.

It is here that we see the major emphasis of the Reformers. They stressed Scripture as the Word of God, the pure unadulterated message from God. They believed Romanism declared that the church is the governor of Scripture, the supreme court with the authority to interpret the charter documents of Christianity. But in the eyes of the Reformers this elevated an interpretation of Scripture over Scripture itself.

In response the Reformers argued for the supremacy of the Scriptures. As Martin Luther wrote, "Neither councils, fathers, nor we, in spite of the greatest and best success possible, will do as well as the Holy Scriptures, that is, as well as God himself has done.... Therefore it behooves us to let the prophets and apostles stand at the professor's lectern, while we, down below at their feet, listen to what they say. It is not they who must hear what we say."[3]

For the Reformers, ultimately there was just one litmus test for a Bible interpretation: did the interpretation point to the gospel of Christ and nurture faith in a gracious God, who through the deeds, shame, suffering and resurrection of Christ had accomplished salvation for us? With this focus Luther outlined in the spring of 1522 how Christians were to read the Gospels. In his treatise *What to Look for and Expect in the Gospels* he reproved Christians who read the Gospels looking only for examples of Christ to imitate.[4] This was certainly one thing to look for, but not the primary thing. Christians, he taught, should read the deeds and sufferings of Christ described in the Gospels as acts performed and endured by Jesus on their behalf, for their salvation. The Gospels are not merely ethical textbooks; they are "gospel," that is, good news about salvation in Christ.

But it is not the Gospels only that have this focus; so too do the New Testament epistles. True, Peter, Paul and others wrote to teach us how to live as Christians. But they also wrote to focus us on the gospel. Even the Old Testament shows forth Christ as both example and gift. This is what the Gospels and the Epistles seek to do—show us who "Christ is, for what purpose he has been given, how he was promised, and how all Scripture tends toward him. For he himself says in [Jn 5:46], 'If you believed Moses, you would also believe me, for he wrote of me.' Again [Jn 5:39], 'search and look up the [Old Testament] Scriptures, for it is they that bear witness of me.'"[5] Luther then reminded his readers of how the New Testament repeatedly leads Christians back to the Old Testament to find Christ.[6]

The Reformers did not intend to find Christ in details of a text that did not specifically mention him. But they were convinced that he is the Bible's central subject, to which everything points and to which all things looked. Calvin said that Christ was represented in all the Old Testament saints and that all the Bible's promises are ultimately fulfilled in him.[7]

Luther and Calvin set forth viewpoints fundamental to Christianity: humanity has a desperate need for salvation provided entirely by God's grace through faith in Christ; humans are saved by a righteousness not their own but Christ's; being Christian means loving your neighbor and being committed to righteous conduct; the church is a community that is to live out its pilgrimage in holy distinction from the world; the interpretation of Scripture must not be confused with Scripture itself; interpretations must always be under the scrutiny of the Bible; and in all their reading, teaching and preaching of the Bible, Christians must hold high Jesus Christ and the gospel.

The issues that we have just studied in the previous three chapters (salvation, church and Scripture) received helpful, crucial definition in the Reformation. But the modern period, which we examine in the last part of our overview, held its own challenges to these doctrines and others. The struggle for purity in belief and practice continued.

Part 4

Chains of Spanish Silver
The Church in the Modern Era

The old craftsman ran the links slowly through his stubby, dirty fingers. He felt the smooth texture, the solid weight of each loop of precious silver mined from the hills of Peru. He gazed at the noble metal's sheen through squinted eyes, drinking in the chain's beauty. The silver chain was a precious piece from the collection of the silversmith Aragon. The old craftsman ran it time after time through his hands, remembering when he, as a much younger man, had been an artisan of the silver from the Cordillera districts. He had formed the malleable metal into ornaments for tableware and jewelry. But never had he seen or touched anything as lovely or perfect as this chain.

But something wasn't right. Three of the chain's pieces, though wonderfully crafted, lacked the luster of the other twenty links. Silver is prized for its ability to reflect 97 percent of visible light, and these three loops appeared dull. The old craftsman's trained eye knew that they were alloys, a mixture of silver and another, less costly metal. That wasn't the mystery. What bothered him was the way in which they had been placed within the chain. Aragon, the maestro, would never have done such an unspeakable thing. Silver chains of Aragon's workmanship always had twenty-five links; this had twenty-three, and not all of them were genuine. This chain was from the hand of Aragon, yet it wasn't. Other hands, less honorable ones, had had their way with the valuable ornament.

The old craftsman knew what he had to do. In the twilight years of life he would renew the chain. He would craft five new links of the purest Cordillera silver. He would restore the hand of Aragon. He would redeem the craftsmanship of his father.

The church has taken some lumps in the modern era (1635–present), but it has also strengthened and introduced themes crucial to true Christianity. The church's faith and practice in the modern era has the same features as Aragon's chain. Links of authentic biblical themes inherited from the orthodoxy of the past are part of the present. But new themes have entered the chain. Some reflect biblical teaching; others are not so biblically based. Restoration of authenticity is still needed. The task of crafting Christianity is still ongoing. We now examine the church in the seventeenth through the twentieth centuries.

The Enlightenment & Modernity

COGITO, ERGO SUM. "I THINK, THEREFORE I AM." With this motto the modern age was off and running. Announced by René Descartes (1596–1650), the French philosopher and mathematician, in his *Discourse on Method* (1637), this maxim dramatically influenced the shape and direction of Western culture, philosophy and theology for almost four hundred years. Descartes was the father of modern rationalism, the belief that reason is the fundamental source for knowing and explaining the world.

In the seventeenth and eighteenth centuries two groups of philosophers offered two different approaches for attaining certain knowledge about the world. The rationalists—Descartes, Benedict de Spinoza (1632–1677) and G. W. F. von Leibniz (1646–1716)—argued that reason must precede experience in the quest for certainty. For the rationalist, information gained through our senses by experience could be misleading. Therefore reason, not experience, was foundational. Simply by thinking, and without experiencing, a person could come to know and explain something.

On the other hand, the empiricists—John Locke (1632–1704), George Berkeley (1685–1753) and David Hume (1711–1776)—stressed that experience was superior to reason in the quest for certainty in knowledge. They said a person needed to experience something through his senses before he could know anything about it. Reason, the use of one's mind, was secondary. A person's mind received information only from her senses.

Both the rationalists and the empiricists have contributed to the spirit of the modern age. The rationalists' emphasis on reason brought forth a skepticism about ancient authorities. Why, people thought, should we rely on an ancient text (the Bible) or a creed since we can discover truth about the world through reason? Why listen to the church? Why listen to anything other than our own rational conclusions?

The empiricists, too, built a foundation that eventually led to skepticism. They had an immense confidence in their experiences as the source of reliable knowledge. This emphasis eventually led people to question the need for ancient authorities. Why do we need the Bible, the church or creeds since our experiences are so trustworthy?

Both movements—rationalism and empiricism—had an overbearing optimism in reason. The only issue was whether it was more important than experience or was secondary to it.

Along with the rationalists and empiricists came the scientific revolution in Western Europe. Even before Descartes, Nicolaus Copernicus (1473–1543) had demonstrated that the earth is spherical and in motion around the sun. This conflicted with the accepted, prevailing, ancient understanding, as codified originally by the ancient Greek astronomer Ptolemy. Similar modifications and rejections of earlier authoritative scientific models came from Galileo Galilei (1564–1642),

Johannes Kepler (1571–1630) and Isaac Newton (1642–1727). The old world's understanding about astronomy and physics was being rejected as misleading and unreliable. Again the modern world nurtured a distrust in ancient authorities. One might say, "If I can't trust Ptolemy, why should I trust *anything* before the fifteenth, or more likely, the eighteenth century?" The modern age was all set to swallow hook, line and sinker an optimism in its ability to figure the world out without relying on ancient authorities.

The Way Things Were

In the early and medieval church three sources had formed the foundation for what people knew to be true: revelation (the Bible), tradition (long-standing doctrines established out of interpretation of Scripture) and reason (the use of the human mind, or careful, logical thinking). Revelation and tradition had run side by side, because tradition guarded against misinterpretations of the Bible. Tradition, for instance, helped oppose the view of the Arians that Christ was created. But tradition was never to replace or supplant revelation. And reason was always subject to, controlled by and limited by revelation and tradition.

In the Reformation, however, a change occurred. Because of what Romanism was teaching about the church and salvation, the Reformers questioned, and in part rejected, the benefits of tradition. But they didn't reject all tradition. They continued to affirm the traditional doctrines of the Trinity and of Christ formulated at the councils of Nicaea, Constantinople and Chalcedon. But they did lose confidence in the accuracy of tradition. And so they began a movement that led to a practical rejection of tradition. Christians, some argued, weren't really helped much by tradition. Left alone with the Bible, one's mind and the Holy Spirit, a Christian could inevitably arrive at the correct interpretation. This wasn't what the Reformers had taught, but this is what became popular. The Reformers had maintained a healthy respect for tradition, but they wanted tradition to be submissive to Scripture. Unfortunately a moderate position was taken to extreme, and tradition lost the day to revelation and reason (the Bible interpreted by one's own mind without any doctrinal guidelines).

The Way Things Became . . . and Are

With the influence of the rationalists, the empiricists and the scientific revolution, the world was set to lose another key source for doctrine. This occurred in a movement of the eighteenth century we call the Enlightenment.

The Enlightenment had various slogans, but they all stressed an overwhelming optimism about the human ability to achieve understanding through reason unattached and unaccountable to any ancient authority. People placed their hope in reason, particularly in the sciences. The Enlightenment magnified a concept defined by Horace, an ancient Latin poet, some eighteen hundred years earlier: "Enlightenment is man's exodus from his self-incurred tutelage."[1] According to Horace, people should be free to use their understanding without being guided by some authority. This idea lay dormant for almost two millennia. Its debut was the Enlightenment.

According to Enlightenment leaders, thinkers in previous centuries had been confined to an intellectual nursery by several harsh, spinster nannies. These were the church, the Bible, creeds, tradition, old scientific theories, the emperor and the pope. But now humanity was grown up and could think and explore on its own.

The motto of Immanuel Kant (1724–1804) was a call for bravery to break away from the nannies: "Dare to know! Have the courage to use your own understanding."[2]

Alexander Pope (1688–1744) poetically set forth the world's hope in science, a hope that emerged in a parody of Genesis 1:

"Nature and Nature's laws lay hid in night; God said 'Let Newton be!' and all was light."[3]

The spirit of the Enlightenment, particularly in its optimistic quest to understand nature, was expressed by Paul Henri Holbach (1723–1789), an atheistic materialist. Denying any spiritual aspect in humans, he declared that humanity is the sole product of nature. True, helpful understanding, he said, comes only through experiential and rational analysis of matter. "Man is unhappy because he is ignorant of Nature."[4]

And theology, which Holbach called "superstition," had hindered people from gaining a happy understanding of nature. Theology was suffocating, for it prevented humanity from gaining the superior knowledge available through experience and reason. "As the born enemy of experience, theology, the science of the supernatural, has been an insuperable obstacle to the progress of the natural sciences. Physics, natural history, and anatomy were not allowed to see anything except through the malevolent eyes of superstition."[5]

With these new expressions of thought, it is no surprise that just as tradition fell in the Reformation, so revelation fell in the Enlightenment. Only reason, separate from any controlling authority, remained on the throne. Everything then became subject to rational argumentation.

Anselm had reflected deep, humble piety in his *Proslogion,* written between 1070 and 1080: "Lord, I am not trying to make my way to your height, for my understanding is in no way equal to that, but I do desire to understand a little of your truth which my heart already believes and loves. I do not seek to understand so that I may believe, but I believe so that I may understand; and what is more, I believe that unless I do believe I shall not understand."[6] But Enlightenment leaders rejected this approach. They asserted that understanding and rationality must precede faith. A person should not consent to believe anything that wasn't first proven reasonable and in line with what could be tested, proven and illustrated from our world.

Whereas Anselm prayerfully confessed, "I believe so that I may understand," the rationalists declared, "I understand in order to believe." And the empiricists proclaimed, "I experience in order to believe." And the scientific revolution announced, "We calculate in order to believe." The inspired teaching of the apostle Paul—"Faith comes from hearing the message, and the message is heard through the word of Christ" (Rom 10:17)—fell on deaf ears in the modern age. Enlightenment people did not heed Isaiah's inspired words that reveal God as the One who shows himself to people who don't seek him and who stumble around blindly in their investigations.

> I revealed myself to those who did not ask for me;
>   I was found by those who did not seek me. . . .
> All day long I have held out my hands
>   to an obstinate people,
> who walk in ways not good,
>   pursuing their own imaginations. (Is 65:1-2)

Also, people influenced by the Enlightenment would have ridiculed the inspired words of Hebrews 11:1-2 —"Now faith is being sure of what we hope for and certain of what we do not see. This is what the ancients were commended for. By faith we understand"—and the many statements in Hebrews 11 about those who lived by faith.

Faith, then, is being certain of something without sensory experience, without seeing, touching, hearing or feeling it. And faith is the basis for understanding. It is not that understanding is a prerequisite for faith. This shouldn't surprise us, because faith comes foremost as a response to revelation, not as a response to reason or experience. Of course, faith isn't irrational or unreasonable, but neither is it founded on reason. Ultimately revelation makes sense, but this side of heaven we can't understand all that God has planned. As Paul said, "For we know in part, . . . but when perfection comes, the imperfect disappears. . . . Now we see but a poor reflection as in a mirror; then [in heaven] we shall see face to face. Now I know in part; then I shall know fully, even as I am fully known" (1 Cor 13:9-12).

Therefore we enter into faith in spite of limited understanding and despite the weakness of our reasoning. Christians attempt to explain the Trinity by various analogies, illustrations or diagrams, but none of them is adequate. Yet we still confess that God eternally exists as one divine essence and three distinct persons. The fact that the Trinity is not easily understood doesn't mean we diminish its importance or deemphasize it in our teaching or preaching. Our inability to comprehend some divine truth completely doesn't mean it is less relevant. Mystery ought not determine practicality. We need to remember that faith is ultimately our submission to God's revelation.

Avery Dulles states that faith is our "surrender of self to God as He reveals himself. . . . The adoring subservience of my whole self to God as supreme Lord of all things. . . . The abandonment of my self-centered vision and my consent to see reality from God's perspective. . . . My grateful resignation of self to God's word in light of his gracious emergence from silence."[7]

In addition to eroding divine revelation as the foundation of faith and mocking tradition, the Enlightenment influenced several Christian doctrines.[8] First, rather than affirming the doctrine of original sin, the Enlightenment denied it and stressed that the idea was oppressive. Humanity needs to be set free not from sin but from *belief* in original sin. Second, rather than affirming the reality of a fallen world tragically affected by sin, Enlightenment people said natural disasters mean that a merciful, sovereign, divine Being does not exist or at least is not involved in the world. Third, they said the Bible is merely a collection of documents without the quality of inspiration. Since the Bible has no divine authorship, it should be interpreted like any other worldly literature. Fourth, the Enlightenment maligned the person of Jesus Christ. It saw his deity as nothing more than the false religious conviction of earlier Christians. In fact, Jesus was merely a superior moral teacher. Clearly, for these eighteenth-century thinkers, he was not God the Son incarnate. Fifth, the Enlightenment leaders twisted the doctrine of salvation, Christ's work on the cross. They said Christ did not die in our place for the penalty of our sins. Instead, he died as an example of self-sacrifice. So people are to be influenced by Jesus' self-giving to give themselves in sacrificial love for others.

The spirit of the Enlightenment didn't disappear; it is still with us today. It has influenced everything in the modern world, even many Christians and churches. Since the eighteenth century, Western culture, in its approach to truth, has been dramatically characterized by the emphases found in the Enlightenment. Let's briefly mention in passing one way in which modernity may have covertly influenced us.

Because of modernity's optimism about knowing anything with certainty from reason, people lack appreciation for history. This failure to appreciate and learn from the past also came through modernity's rejection of ancient authorities. If we, on our own, can know complete truth now, then what people thought in the past is irrelevant. What is most recent is best.

Of course, all of these characteristics of the Enlightenment would impact spirituality. But happily, as our next chapter shows, the eighteenth century also saw the awakening ministry of the Holy Spirit.

9

Awakenings
& Revivals

THE ENLIGHTENMENT EVENTUALLY cooled the fires of the Reformation in Europe. But in the midst of the Age of Reason, the Reformation was already cooling for other reasons. The primary reason was formalism. Given time and the nature of humanity, even the themes of the Reformers had become routine. Many in Europe and the new American colonies were Protestant, but even Protestantism was experiencing a coldness, a deadness, a stagnancy. In many sectors it had become nothing more than conventional orthodoxy. Thus two arrows had pierced the chest of the Reformation: reason and ritual. It was popular to believe that salvation was simply a matter of giving assent to orthodox beliefs or behaving morally.

Spiritual Awakening in the Eighteenth Century
In Europe and America, both of which had sunk deep in reason and ritual, a wheel of revival began to turn in the early part of the eighteenth century. With European Pietism as its roots, the revival

owed some of its flavor to Lutheran Pietists like Philipp Jakob Spener (1635–1705) and the Moravian Pietist Nikolaus Ludwig von Zinzendorf (1700–1760). The Pietists, though coming from different traditions, had similar themes of emphasis. Against laxity in spiritual fervor and morality, the Pietists stressed conversion, the study of the Scriptures in small groups, the singing of hymns and prayer. They deemphasized doctrine, the creeds and certain particulars of theology. Their feeling toward doctrine turned on the belief that doctrine and careful theological thinking had not kept the church devotionally zealous. This attitude of the Pietists was unfortunate but somewhat understandable, given the spiritual depression of the times. The Pietists yearned for warmth, for a heart of flesh and not of stone.

Also influencing the revival of the eighteenth century was Puritanism. Generally classed as a group from within the Church of England who sought to purify that church, the Puritans brought their convictions to the New World. They, too, emphasized the important theme of a conversion experience by grace, along with an extraordinary emphasis on the preaching of the Scriptures, as the rule of faith and practice.

The First Great Awakening was conceived in New Jersey under the evangelical ministry of Theodore Frelinghuysen (1691–1747), a Dutch Reformed pastor. Under his preaching the eyelids of revival began to flutter in the 1720s, although the full Awakening didn't take place until the 1730s and 1740s. In the 1720s and 1730s the Tennent family (mostly William and his son Gilbert) brought revival to the Presbyterian churches of Pennsylvania and New Jersey. Jonathan Edwards (1703–1758) was used of God in 1734 and 1735 to awaken Northampton, Massachusetts, spiritually. In the preaching tours of George Whitefield (1714–1770) in the 1740s, sleepy souls of New England were led into full spiritual consciousness. In particular, during 1740 Whitefield preached 175 sermons to thousands in a marathon forty-five-day itinerant preaching tour.

This wonderfully gifted Calvinistic speaker could attract and hold the attention of virtually anyone. Preferring narrative portions of Scripture, Whitefield painted captivating, imaginative word pictures of heaven, hell, humanity's desperate need for Christ and conversion through faith as the dramatic change in one's affections and life orientation from self to God. In the 1750s, through the ministries of those like Samuel Davies (1723–1761) in Virginia and Shubal Stearns (1706–1771) in North Carolina, the South, too, would know revival.

Much skepticism about the Awakening's authenticity arose. Critics questioned its emotionalism and were irritated by the disruptions it brought to the religious norm. Its greatest defender was Jonathan Edwards.

Edwards preached over twelve hundred sermons, and his series on justification by faith opened the revival among his congregation in Northampton. From Jesus' words of blessing to Peter in Matthew 16:17 Edwards preached a famous sermon entitled "A Divine and Supernatural Light." This sermon, first preached in 1734, explained the crucial theology behind the truth that Peter was given his faith in Christ not from "flesh and blood" but by God the Father in heaven. Edwards believed that "spiritual knowledge," or knowledge of Jesus' identity as the Christ, the Son of God, had no human messenger. God alone is its author by the revealing ministry of the Spirit of God. A person may become religiously interested because of a message spoken by another person, but this would not be "spiritual light" or "spiritual discovery." For when one has been "spiritually enlightened," a transformation of heart and mind has taken place. "He don't [*sic*] merely rationally believe that God is glorious, but he has a sense of the gloriousness of God in his heart. There is not only a rational belief that God is holy, and that holiness is a good thing; but there is a sense of the loveliness of God's holiness."[1]

Such an appreciation of God, Edwards believed, could come

only through a radical work of God's Spirit. We are unable to work up such a perspective. And such a sincere attraction to God's beauty is at the root of conversion. Conversion is not merely about "getting saved"; it is not simply uttering a short prayer. Conversion is about a new way, an enlightened way, the true way, of seeing God and his Word. And this way of seeing God comes only from him. And yet for Edwards such faith, such a conversion of mind and heart, is not irrational. He said it is rational to believe that God as the divine Being is supreme in his glory; it is rational to suppose that such glory could be seen to some degree by some; and it is rational to suppose that such seeing would be provided only by God himself and not by flesh and blood. One can almost hear Edwards saying within the Age of Enlightenment that true enlightenment is not breaking away from ancient authorities to reason but receiving an in-breaking of God to the eyes of our hearts.

Edwards also addressed the signs of a true revival. In the treatise *The Distinguishing Marks of a Work of the Spirit of God* (written in 1741, the same year of his famous sermon "Sinners in the Hands of an Angry God") Edwards identified several criteria for authentic awakening, based on 1 John 4:1-21.[2] First, against his critics he established the things that do not nullify true revival, including irregular moral conduct and dramatic emotional responses. A true work of God's Spirit does not mean that at conversion a person becomes instantly or totally holy. Nor should we doubt true conversion if it was highly emotional and accompanied with tears, groans or outcries. Second, Edwards pointed out five clear evidences of actual conversion: (1) a conviction that Jesus is the incarnate, virgin-born, crucified Son of God and Savior of sinful humans (1 Jn 4:2-3); (2) a developing disinterest in, and a weaning away from, worldly lusts and pursuits, accompanied by an affection for the supremacy of things divine and heavenly (1 Jn 4:4-5); (3) an appreciation and higher regard for the Scriptures, the Bible (1 Jn 4:6); (4) a truthful view of things regarding God, sin and self (1 Jn 4:6); and (5) a growing love for God and fellow humans (1 Jn 4:7-21).

This last one especially captivated Edwards. He wrote, "In these verses [1 Jn 4:12-13] love is spoken of as if it were that wherein the very nature of the Holy Spirit consisted; or, as if divine love dwelling in us, and the Spirit of God dwelling in us were the same thing. . . . Therefore this last mark which the apostle gives of the true Spirit he seems to speak of as the most eminent; and so insists much more largely upon it, than upon all the rest."[3]

These are remarkable words. The Spirit's indwelling of the believer and his or her love for God and neighbor go together. That is, the one who has the Spirit loves. What does this love look like? The answer, according to Edwards, focuses on two words: delight and humility.

If I truly love God, I delight in contemplating the glory, perfection and loveliness of his divine attributes. I admire our Lord Jesus Christ and find him altogether beautiful. I conform my will to God's will, so that I am pleasing to him. If I love my fellow humans, I renounce myself, abase myself, empty myself. While I exalt God's loveliness and perform acts of kindness toward others, I renounce my own qualities, denying my own desires. Such love comes only as a true work of the Holy Spirit within the one who has known the rich, free, sovereign grace of God.

Perhaps Edwards's most developed understanding of the essence of spiritual revival is presented in his work *A Treatise Concerning Religious Affections*, written in 1746. There he stated, "True religion in great part, consists in holy affections."[4] By "affections" he meant the virtues imparted to us supernaturally through the indwelling of the Holy Spirit, what Paul called "the fruit of the Spirit" (Gal 5:22). These are not supplementary to conversion, Edwards said; they are the essence of conversion. For true religion, he believed, one needs both light and heat.

That is, in conversion one comes to perceive and understand the truth about God and Christ through the Spirit's gracious work. But also the Spirit impacts one's inclination, that is, one's will, heart and affections. The converted person receives a new understanding (light) and a new "affected fervented heart."[5] These are not natural; they cannot be cooked up or built up by a rigorous disciplined life. They are accomplished spiritually by the divine Spirit, and they are exercised in Christian faith and practice.

Edwards was optimistic about the transforming power of grace, for it gives new understanding, new affection and new Christian actions. He wrote that "true grace is not an unactive thing; there is nothing in heaven or earth of a more active nature.... 'Tis no barren thing; there is nothing in the universe that in its nature has a greater tendency to fruit. Godliness in the heart has as direct a relation to practice, as a fountain has to a stream, or as the luminous nature of the sun has to beams sent forth."[6]

We can see from these brief glances at the teachings of Jonathan Edwards that he was a theologian of revival. Careful doctrinal contemplation of how God works in revival, what revival consists of and where it should lead did not get buried in the drama of revival. Understanding revival theologically was not somehow peripheral to revival; it was integral with it.

We can also see that Edwards was strongly God-centered in his view of revival. True revival was wholly a gracious, transforming work of God. It was not essentially method, system, leadership, strategy or tactic. God's powerful grace—and no human creativity, effort or ingenuity—was at the bedside of authentic awakening.

Revival also came to Great Britain. Its initial period occurred approximately between 1715 and 1735. It blossomed over the next forty years. The choice for a key figure is not difficult. It falls without argument to John Wesley (1703–1791), the founder of Methodism. Wesley had been drawn to the faith and sense of gracious, personal salvation through Christ evident among the Moravians. This was a pietistic community consisting of refugees from Moravia, with some loyalties to German Lutheranism. They had challenged him to seek his own personal forgiveness and redemption. Wesley's testimony to his own conversion on May 24, 1738, which took place during a reading of Luther's preface to his *Commentary on Romans,* reflects these themes. This experience of grace guided him to dedicate himself to the work of evangelism in order to bring divine life to human souls. He preached well into his eighties, traveling untold miles on horseback. The great fruit of his evangelistic ministry led to his organization of "societies," the first in London in 1739. Originally a Moravian device, societies were intended to methodically foster holiness in the lives of the converted. Wesley willingly maintained his ministry within the Church of England. It was only after his death that differences over church government, in particular the issues of ordination and ministerial authority to administer the sacraments, resulted in separation of the Methodists from the Church of England.

Doctrinally, Wesley was not as Calvinistic as his counterparts ministering in colonial America, and he and Whitefield had strong differences of opinion over predestination. Wesley believed in a gracious restoration of free will within fallen humanity and was convinced that redeemed humans were capable of a level of perfect sanctification in this life. Like his counterparts in colonial America, however, Wesley spearheaded a renewal of God's converting grace through Christ in a time when religious culture substituted for conversion and hearts were cold.

Nineteenth-Century Revivalism

The wheels of revival began to turn again in America a generation or so after Edwards's ministry. Beginning toward the end of the eighteenth century, this series of revivals, known as the Second Great Awakening, differs from the First of the 1740s particularly in theological emphasis. Geographically the Second Awakening reached beyond New England to the south and west. It was diverse in character and location. Theologian and Yale president Timothy Dwight (1752–1817) is counted among its proponents, yet Tennessee and Kentucky were among its most flamboyant centers. It occurred within universities but also within the camp meetings that so quickly became the hallmark medium of frontier revivals. Congregationalists took the early lead, but soon Baptists, Presbyterians and Methodists were also participants. It served as fertile ground for the planting and growth of societies that advocated missions, education (Christian and secular), the abolition of slavery, women's rights and pacifism.

Theologically, while the First Awakening had maintained a strong Calvinistic heritage, the Second was more sympathetic to an Arminian tone. Traced back to Jacob Arminius (1560–1690), Arminianism was a movement within the Dutch Reformed Church that rejected the Calvinistic emphases on predestination and irresistible grace. In classic Arminianism God did not foreordain the election of some to faith. Instead, he elected through foreknowledge those who would respond freely to grace. Calvinism, on the other hand, taught that God has sovereignly foreordained some (the elect) to believe.

Also according to Arminianism, God provides prevenient grace, which enables the fallen human will to respond freely to grace. The human will can freely cooperate with grace and believe or freely refuse to cooperate and not believe. Calvinism, however, emphasized salvation as entirely an act of God from start to finish. The elect will believe because God foreordained it. In Arminianism receiving grace is conditional on people's free response, but in Calvinism God's grace is irresistible.

For the Second Great Awakening and Charles G. Finney (1792–1875), who was both one of its products and one of its representatives, revival was largely an issue of method, tactic and technique. The evangelists employed strategies aimed at developing an atmosphere in which dramatic conversions could be provoked. The camp meetings that took place in the frontier areas provided such an environment. They were held in areas remote from towns or cities, where hundreds of people were confined in close quarters for several days, listening to repetitive gospel messages and appeals for decision.

Finney employed several means to elicit decisions, two of which were the anxious bench and the protracted meeting. Listeners who felt that they were on the verge of conversion would come forward and sit on the anxious bench until their degree of anxiety reached critical level. This heightened anxiety would hopefully end their struggle and encourage them to decide to submit to the gospel. The protracted meeting was usually a regionally or communally confined meeting, lasting several weeks in urban areas. Finney intended the continual pressure from the community to aid in bringing about dramatic surrender to his message.

Finney's methods were strongly linked to his theology. For Finney, a revival was not a miracle, for nothing in religion lay beyond ordinary laws of nature.[7] Humans who became spiritually alive were not supernaturally enabled to become something they had been unable to be before. Revival was simply humans freely using natural powers in ways that glorified God. Therefore he believed that revival could be brought about through proper use of means. In his 1835 lectures given in New York City and published under the title *Lectures on Revivals of Religion,* Finney argued in favor of these natural means to revival. There he defined revival as "a purely philosophical result of the right use of the constituted means—as much so as any other effect produced by the application of means."[8] For

Finney, God's sovereignty in the operation of gracious salvation is the same as God's sovereignty in nature. They both happen within natural systems of cause and effect. Certain means usually (if not always) produce distinct results. God's way of revival wasn't arbitrary to Finney.

This view of things, of course, was linked to his belief that humans are free moral agents. Finney taught that conversion is something people are totally capable of doing themselves. In a sermon preached in 1835, "Sinners Bound to Change Their Own Hearts," he set forth the following theses from Ezekiel 18:31, which contains the phrase "get a new heart and a new spirit": "We have the powers of moral agency. . . . We do not need to be altered in soul or body; we do not need to add to our minds any new principle. . . . The new heart and the new spirit is not a constitutional change in our human nature. . . . The change of heart Ezekiel spoke of is not miraculous, it is just a choice we make to employ our abilities in obedience to God rather than in self-gratification."[9] This is why Finney believed that revival comes about by various strategies to provoke individuals into using their hearts for God rather than for self or Satan.

Against this background of free moral agency and denial of human bondage to sin, Finney's view of the atonement also differed from that of the leaders of the First Awakening. He did not preach the crucifixion of Christ as a penal substitutionary atonement. That is, Christ did not suffer in our place as our substitute, bearing on himself our punishment. Rather, Finney preached what is called a governmental and moral influence view of the atonement. In his sermon "On the Atonement" he announced that Christ "was not punished."[10] Christ's death made a governmental statement. It testified to God's high regard for the law, which had been broken by sin, and his hatred for sin. At the cross God gave "a demonstration of His attitude toward sin."[11] But Jesus' death also served another purpose. It manifested such a high degree of "love, meekness, and self-sacrifice for us" that it makes us "bow before the cross with a broken and contrite heart."[12] When a sinner understands the cross, it should break his or her heart and cause conversion in the sinner's will. For Finney, since conversion was only a matter of a person by his or her own will choosing God, the cross was an influence on the will.

In the revivalism of the Second Awakening and the American Christianity that developed from it, crisis conversions became identified as the essence of Christianity. That is part of Christianity, but it isn't all of it. Along with crisis conversions came a strong individualism. This stress on a private, personal faith led to a failure to embrace a faith shared in common by the believing community. Furthermore, revivalism fostered antitraditionalism and an infatuation with the present. Spiritual formation was associated with the instantaneous and the contemporary. The beliefs and practices of Christians in the past were irrelevant for spirituality in the present. The virtue of thinking Christianly in association with the Christian community of all eras was consumed by an individual, crisis experience of the present. As Mark Noll has written, "American revivalism did much to hamstring the life of the mind."[13]

A movement connected to revivalism in general, and to the holiness emphasis of Wesley and the transformed-life emphasis of Finney in particular, began to take root before the dawn of the twentieth century.[14] Pentecostalism emphasized a second crisis experience after conversion as normative and advanced the belief that the Holy Spirit's power, evidenced by gifts in the New Testament era, was again being outpoured. The second blessing, the filling of the Spirit, was witnessed to by the ability to speak in tongues and the possession of other spiritual gifts listed by Paul (1 Cor 12).

It is with a revival in 1906 that we can associate the dynamic inauguration of Pentecostalism. William J. Seymour (1870–

1922), an African American minister of a gospel mission on Azusa Street in Los Angeles, California, began the fundamental revivals. The movement, emphasizing the Spirit, sign gifts, supernaturalism, evangelism, worship, Bible study and social sympathies, although starting slowly, developed into one of the largest movements of twentieth-century Christianity. The emphases of the movement brought forth Pentecostal denominations (for example, Assemblies of God) and found adherents within all mainline Protestant denominations and Roman Catholicism (charismatic Christians).

Pentecostals and charismatics now have an astounding global presence and representation, numbering 524 million worldwide. Their influence on the Third World has been extraordinary.

Liberalism, Missions & Evangelicalism

As THE MODERN AGE PROGRESSED, some Christians grew more and more skeptical about the feasibility of ancient orthodox beliefs in the modern, critical world. Could they preach the old, old story in a new, new world in which the way of thinking was supposedly more sophisticated than in the early, medieval or Reformation worlds? Would the modern world accept traditional beliefs like the Trinity, the unity of Jesus in two natures, the total depravity of humans and the penal, substitutionary atonement? Or did these older beliefs need to be modified in order to find acceptance in the modern world?

Nineteenth-Century Liberalism
Nineteenth-century Protestant liberals opted for severe modification of the traditional faith. They viewed themselves as the saviors of a defunct, out-of-date Christianity. They would make Christianity palatable to a mindset that could no longer accept traditional orthodoxy. This modification of Christian beliefs

took place in one of two ways—they were either dismissed entirely or were reinterpreted in a way that would make them acceptable to the modern worldview. In the opinion of liberals, modern thought had made many new claims into which traditional Christianity had to be assimilated. Authorities other than the Bible would be pivotal within this agenda. Reason, culture, experience and science would all be employed in challenge to the classical authority of revelation. These sources would also be employed in criticism of traditional faith claims such as those found in the orthodox creeds.

The father of modern liberalism was the German theologian Friedrich Schleiermacher (1768–1834). His two most famous works, *On Religion: Speeches to Its Cultured Despisers* (1799) and *The Christian Faith* (1821–1822; rev. ed. 1830), set the tone for an era. The former text argued to the disenchanted that religion was not subservience to the orthodox dogma or moralism of bygone times. Authentic religion was an immediate, universal human feeling. The latter book was a systematic presentation of theology in keeping with Schleiermacher's thoroughly modern approach.

Schleiermacher defined the true essence of religion as the feeling of being absolutely dependent on God. Feeling does not mean a mere emotion or a sensation of pleasure or pain. It is an overwhelming consciousness that a person is in a relationship with God. This relationship is defined totally by the person's self-conscious dependence on God.

In this way Schleiermacher believed theology was not so much one's reflection on Scripture as one's reflection on his or her experience of God. He did not view traditional, authoritative doctrines, creeds and biblical texts as the preeminent sources in theology. Instead, he taught that a person's self-consciousness and feeling of God gave rise to religious concepts. For him, religious experience replaced doctrines and antiquated ethical credos. Permanent validity was the property of human religious consciousness, not of archaic, transient formulas. Likewise, he did not regard the culturally bound literature of the Bible as normative.

Hand in hand with his understanding of religion and feeling went his concept of God. God is a sovereign power, believed Schleiermacher, but God is not to be separated from the world. God is immanent in everything. The theologian's refusal to objectify God is consistent with his subjective approach to religion. True religion is not outside the human but within the human's self-consciousness—that is, the subject's experience.

For Schleiermacher, Christianity was the premier religion because of Jesus Christ. Jesus is unique because of the great extent of his God-consciousness. More than any other person, Christ had the feeling of being dependent on God. For this reason, Schleiermacher was a Christian rather than a Jew, a Hindu or a Muslim. He was a follower of Christ because Christ was the most religious person who ever lived.

Schleiermacher reduced Christianity to a single aspect: the romantic notion of *feeling*. In rejecting doctrine as Christianity's center Schleiermacher erased the real God-man, reducing Jesus Christ to a religious person. And this set a pattern for liberalism's later proponents. Liberalism was usually reductive; that is, it tried to reduce the essence of Christianity to a least-common denominator that anyone in the modern world could accept.

Although Schleiermacher was liberalism's father, its most classic, influential expression came with Albrecht Ritschl (1822–1889). His main literary contribution was *The Christian Doctrine of Justification and Reconciliation* in three volumes (1870–1874). For Ritschl, the essence of religion was not to objectify God or to reflect upon God in his being. He believed, rather, that authentic religion concerned itself only with value judgments or knowledge about God that had a moral effect and thereby contributed to humanity's greatest good. Ultimately he identified God with his effects in relation to humans rather than with his own holy being. The value of metaphysical expressions of God, such as in the creed of Nicaea, was lost for Ritschl, since they substituted the scientific and theoretical for religion.

Paramount in Ritschl's mind was the kingdom of God, humanity in loving unity. God as love revealed in Jesus was the only important divine attribute, and it found progressive manifestation in the kingdom. Thus Christianity is fundamentally an ethical reality where Christians complete this ideal of love. In keeping with Ritschl's system, then, Christ is not ultimately the God-man of Chalcedon, for that would be of purely scientific interest. Jesus is valued for his ethical, religious character. Any view of his divinity rests not in his nature but in the unique ethical commitment he gives to God. Christ is basically a moral example and inspiration.

The challenge for contemporary Christians with traditional, orthodox loyalties is to remain faithful in three things: (1) the confession that revelation is essentially outside of us in the Bible and in Jesus Christ, the incarnate Son of the Trinity; (2) faithful reflection on God in his being as he is in his holy immensity; and (3) living in a manner, by the Holy Spirit, that is consistent with Jesus' ethical teaching. Karl Barth (1886–1968), a Swiss Reformed pastor and theologian, emphasized the first of the three. Against liberal Protestantism he stressed that because of humanity's depravity, humans are fully dependent upon the revelation of the supreme, transcendent God in Jesus Christ, the Word of God. A religion based in subjective experience is impossible. God is other. God is not a universal, human consciousness. Barth began his polemic with his *Commentary on Romans* (1919) and systematized his theology in the thirteen volumes of his *Church Dogmatics* (1932–1967).

Nineteenth-century Protestant liberalism was not confined

to Europe. Henry Ward Beecher (1813–1887), a pastor in Brooklyn, said that the old, old story just wouldn't do. In a lecture at Yale University in 1872 he argued that the intellectual sophistication of the modern world could no longer accept the ancient doctrines. They had to be modified in line with the progress of understanding or else pastors would become preachers of a dead past: "There is being now applied among Scientists a greater amount of real, searching, discriminating thought . . . than ever has been expended . . . in the whole history of the world put together. . . . If ministers do not make their theological systems conform to the facts as they are . . . the time will not be far distant when the pulpit will be like a voice crying in the wilderness."[1]

In the American brand of Protestant liberalism, emphasis was placed on the nature of the Bible. American theologians like Augustus Hopkins Briggs (1841–1913) created doubt about the Scriptures' complete trustworthiness. At his 1891 inauguration into the chair of biblical studies at Union Theological Seminary, Briggs delivered an address entitled "The Authority of Holy Scripture." In the address he denied the verbal inspiration and inerrancy of Scripture. In his book *The Bible, the Church and the Reason,* published a year later, he denied that the truths of Scripture extend to its very words or expressions. In 1924 Shailer Matthews (1863–1941) ferried the liberal view into the twentieth century. In his book *Faith of Modernism* he stated the agenda of modern liberalism clearly: "The Modernist is deliberately undertaking to adjust Christianity to modern needs by changing the emphasis in its message and by historically evaluating and restating the permanent significance of evangelical Christianity to human life."[2]

For Matthews, orthodox doctrines needed radical restatement within the categories established by the physical sciences, history and sociology of his day. The doctrines established by the early church, and even by the Reformation, do not have permanent validity. They were significant only for those moments in history. Matthews sought to "adjust" Christianity by making it more palatable for the modern day.

Modern Protestant Missions: Finally an International Church
Though revivalism and liberalism characterized the nineteenth century, European colonialism and the promotion of Protestant missions also occurred during that period. Like the revivals we have studied, Protestant missions have an essential relationship to the Pietism of the eighteenth century. They also had an essential relationship to colonialism.

The father of modern missions is usually identified as William Carey (1761–1834). Carey himself, however, was well aware of his predecessors in the great work. A Baptist pastor in England, Carey became heavily burdened for the unevangelized. At a meeting of ministers in Leicester in 1792 he preached a missionary sermon entitled "Expect Great Things from God; Attempt Great Things for God." Later that same year the Baptist Missionary Society was founded, due in large part to Carey's efforts. As its first missionary, Carey left for Bengal, India, the next year. He immersed himself in Bible translation, evangelism and pastoring. In 1800 he moved to Serampore, where he extended his ministry to include church planting and teaching. Carey did not isolate himself from the larger world. He saw the need to integrate missionary vision into various avenues of life as a whole. He worked at providing medical services, produced a Bengali-English dictionary and founded the Agricultural and Horticultural Society of India. Although the Baptist Missionary Society concentrated its work in India, later it sponsored work in Jamaica, China, the Cameroons and Congo.

For British Christians in the nineteenth century, missionary vision and spirit was in close relationship with social concerns and issues of freedom and dignity in keeping with the Christian view of humanity. Therefore, it is no surprise to learn that David Livingstone's (1813–1873) labor in Africa was influenced by his conviction that commerce and Christianity within that country would diminish the slave trade. He first arrived under the London Missionary Society in 1840 and died thirty-three years later in Zambia. As a missionary and explorer, he carried out the vision of a devout evangelical member of the British Parliament. William Wilberforce (1759–1833), in addition to his duties in Parliament, was a member of the Clapham sect, a group made up of wealthy Anglican evangelicals. Wilberforce and the other members of the sect mobilized against slavery and witnessed the abolition of the slave trade throughout Britain and its colonies initially in 1807 and ultimately in 1833. The Clapham sect also had a hand in founding the Society for Missions in Africa and the East (1799), which in 1812 became the Church Missionary Society (CMS) and, in 1995, the Church Mission Society. It was the first effective Anglican missionary association.

In America, Samuel J. Mills (1783–1818) was largely responsible for a focus on foreign missions. In 1810 he and Adoniram Judson (1788–1850), along with other students from Andover Seminary, helped form the first American foreign missionary society, named the American Board of Commissioners for Foreign Missions (ABCFM). Congregationalist in affiliation, the ABCFM also sponsored missionaries from other denominations, and in 1961 it became the United Church Board for World Ministries (UCBWM), a missionary arm of the United Church of Christ. The ABCFM and UCBWM concentrated efforts in Hawaii, China, India, Sri Lanka, Japan, southern Africa, Turkey and Syria. Other denominationally affiliated missionary groups formed in the nineteenth century include the American Baptist Missionary Union (1814) and the Presbyterian Board (1837).

The story behind the forming of the ABCFM is interesting.

Many of the students at Andover Seminary who were instrumental in founding this mission had previously studied at Williams College in Massachusetts, where they regularly met for prayer. In the summer of 1806, while they were in prayer at one of their meetings, a thunderstorm forced them to take shelter under a haystack. It was during this hour of prayer that the members of the group committed themselves to praying fervently for overseas missions. Known as the "Haystack Prayer Meeting," it is frequently highlighted as the pivotal event in the founding of American foreign missions.

In addition to denominationally sponsored missions there also arose faith missions. These groups were independently founded and were nondenominational or interdenominational. One of these was the China Inland Mission (1865), founded by J. Hudson Taylor (1832–1905). Working within the interior of China, Taylor exemplified "becoming Chinese so that he might reach the Chinese." He also practiced full dependence on God and his people for daily and ministerial needs. Renamed the Overseas Missionary Fellowship in 1965, this mission ministers in several regions of Asia. In the latter part of the nineteenth century the Christian and Missionary Alliance (1886), the Central American Mission (1890) and The Evangelical Alliance Mission (1890) were founded.

With this nineteenth-century background, Christians were well prepared for the Edinburgh World Missionary Conference of 1910. This conference was needed because of the great unfinished task of evangelization. Over the previous 110 years the world's Christian population had increased 10 percent. At the beginning of the twentieth century just under 35 percent of the world was identified as Christian. Over half the world still remained untouched by evangelism.[3]

Though the conference was not earthshaking in its missionary fruit, it portrayed the twentieth century's recognition of the international dimensions of the Christian faith—a recognition that had dawned largely because of missionary efforts in the previous century. The conference represented the first time that denominations and missionary societies had joined in congress with an agenda and had attempted to divide up international missionary responsibilities. It gave birth to the International Missionary Council (IMC) and inaugurated the movement toward establishing the World Council of Churches (WCC). Although Edinburgh gave place on the program to churches from the Third World, the dimensions of Christianity in 1910 were restrictively Western and the vision was not as comprehensively global as in later conventions.

In 1974 international missions would be the topic of another pivotal conference. The Lausanne Congress on World Evangelization met for ten days with almost twenty-five hundred participants from 150 countries. Convened by Billy Graham, it delivered a comprehensive level of global attention and conditioned the future approaches of modern missions toward people groups rather than toward nations. Demography became the issue of definition instead of geography. Donald A. McGavran (1897–1991) and Ralph D. Winter (1924–) were paradigm-creating forces in this focus. The congress spawned the Lausanne Committee for World Evangelization (LCWE), which continues the work of the congress in a manner consistent with the Lausanne Covenant, the document representative of the principles of the meeting <www.lausanne.org>. Those principles include, among others, the unity of evangelism and social concern, cooperation within Christianity's diversity, the Holy Spirit's centrality to missions and the uniqueness of Christ.

The success of missions in the last century was greatly aided by the availability of Bible translations. William Carey was instrumental in the beginning of the work, and we should not forget Robert Morrison's (1782–1834) publication of his Chinese Bible in 1823. Wycliffe Bible Translators International

(WBTI) continues their early work. Founded in 1934 by William Cameron Townsend (1896–1982), WBTI is an international group committed to providing vernacular translations to all the world's peoples. Some two thousand minority languages, they estimate, still require translations of the Bible. The good news is that in 1995 the number of languages into which the entire Bible had been translated numbered almost 350. This is up from only 105 in 1950. For just the New Testament, in 1995, available translations numbered 841, up from 229 in 1950.[4]

Today, we must speak of global missions and a global Christianity. The new edition of the *World Christian Encyclopedia* notes: "During the 20th century, . . . Christianity has become the most extensive and universal religion in history. There are today Christians and organized Christian churches in every inhabited country on earth. The church is therefore now, for the first time in history, ecumenical in the literal meaning of the word: its boundaries are coextensive with the *oikumene,* the whole inhabited world."[5] Two-Thirds World missions—the missionary pursuits of the countries of Latin America, Africa, Asia and Oceania—sent forth an estimated eighty-eight thousand workers from sixteen hundred agencies in the mid-1990s.[6] Twenty years earlier the count was fewer than three thousand missionaries. The number of Christians in the non-Western world has exploded as well. In 1900 there were 8.8 million Christians in Africa. Today there are 335 million. The figures are just as astounding for Asia (20.7 million in 1900; 307.3 million today), Latin America (60 million in 1900; 475.7 million today) and Oceania (4.3 million in 1900; 21.4 million today).

In the year 2000 the majority of Christians were outside the Western continents of Europe and North America. In fact, 60 percent of Christians are now from the Two-Thirds World: Africa (18 percent); Asia (16 percent); Latin America (25 percent); Oceania (1 percent). Europe claims just over 28 percent of the world's Christian population, and North America not even 12 percent. This is a dramatic shift from 1900, when 71 percent of Christians were European and only 2 percent, 4 percent and 12 percent were African, Asian and Latin American, respectively. The Third World has become the center of Christianity, and as it looks to the remainder of this century, it desperately needs two things: (1) the further mobilization of national Christians for the continued Christianization of their own nations (indigenization and contextualization); and (2) the training of the numerous, newly converted laity.

Not only has the Christian world changed shape, but the missionary efforts over the last century have reduced the unevangelized population of the world from 54 percent to 27 percent. The last thirty years alone have witnessed a 14 percent reduction. All of this is in keeping with the heartbeat of the Christian Scriptures, which tell of the God who desires, and the church that should labor for, the globalization of Christianity.

> Declare his glory among the nations,
>   his marvelous deeds among all peoples. (Ps 96:3)

> Go and make disciples of all nations. (Mt 28:19)

Yes, Christianity is the world's largest religion as the twenty-first century begins (2 billion), and great leaps in fulfilling the Great Commission have taken place. However, 66 percent of the world's population is non-Christian. Despite the progress in evangelization and Bible translation, 4 billion souls this year are without Christ. For 2025 the projection is 5 billion.

But before leaving the topics of the advancement and remaining need of missions in the twentieth century, one other issue must be mentioned: mission and society. The twentieth century witnessed some progress here as well, yet Christians still face the enduring challenges of soothing suffering and implementing social justice. In Dublin, Bengal and Calcutta one thinks of Mother Teresa (1910–1997) of the Missionaries of Charity, ministering to the poor, sick and dying. Recipient of the Nobel Peace Prize for 1979, she exemplified self-giving in an age of commercialism. The archbishop of Cape Town, Desmond Tutu (1931–), was overwhelmingly important as a critic and activist against apartheid in South Africa, receiving the Nobel Peace Prize in 1984.

In twentieth-century America the churches and society were still plagued by the racial tension that had begun much earlier in the nation's history. Richard Allen (1760–1831), for instance, had experienced the forces of segregation in the Methodist Episcopal Church in the 1780s. This led to his founding the African Methodist Episcopal Church (AMEC). Born into slavery but eventually able to purchase his freedom, Allen was gifted in ministry. African Americans flocked to his services at St. George's Methodist Church, Philadelphia, a predominantly white congregation. This influx of black worshipers, however, resulted in increased racial tension and segregation within St. George's. In response Allen and his followers withdrew and started a congregation known as the Free African Society. Allen emphasized the social and economic concerns inherent in anything called Christian. In 1793 he established the Bethel African Methodist Episcopal Church, Philadelphia. Francis Asbury (1745–1816), the first Methodist bishop in America, performed the dedication, but the AMEC was only established in 1816.

In the twentieth century things had improved little if at all. In an environment of pervasive social injustice Martin Luther King Jr. (1929–1968) became the visible, leading voice against racial discrimination through nonviolence. Assassinated in Memphis, Tennessee, on April 4, 1968, at the age of thirty-nine, King had rallied the conscience of the nation against the practice of segregation, the tolerance of poverty and the furtherance of war. The son of a Baptist minister, King had been touched by the evangelical spirituality of that African American tradition as well as by his experience at Morehouse College, the ideology at Boston University (where he earned his Ph.D. in

1955) and the pacifism of Gandhi. Common within his ecclesiological tradition, King's convictions united theology and struggle, faith and social justice. In his leadership of the civil rights movement he challenged America to make this unity part of a national paradigm. He served as pastor and associate pastor, led the bus boycott in Montgomery in 1955 and 1956, and in 1957 helped organize the Southern Christian Leadership Conference (SCLC), which advocates reform in civil rights by nonviolent means. He became president of the SCLC in 1957. From 1962 to 1965 King helped organize and lead several major campaigns. In 1963 he made two of his most moving statements. Jailed in Birmingham, he eloquently defended his ministry in his "Letter from Birmingham Jail—April 16, 1963." He delivered his "I Have a Dream" speech at the march on Washington the same year. His activities contributed to the legislative success of the Civil Rights Act (1964) and the Voting Rights Act (1965). He was awarded the Nobel Peace Prize in 1964, and in 1986 Congress made his birthday—January 15, 1929—a national holiday (celebrated the third Monday in January).

> Hate evil, love good,
> And establish justice in the gate!
> I hate, I reject your festivals,
> Nor do I delight in your solemn assemblies.
> Take away from me the noise of your songs;
> I will not even listen to the sound of your harps.
> But let justice roll down like waters
> And righteousness like an ever-flowing stream.
> (Amos 5:15, 21, 23-24, NASB)

Evangelicalism

Arising out of the eighteenth-century revivals taking place in Britain and the British colonies, evangelicalism is a movement essentially connected to Puritanism and Pietism. American evangelicalism, with its own distinctive history, looks back to its British footing and continues to experience important influence from the evangelicalism of England. Throughout the world today there are 211 million evangelicals. Five convictions are at the base of the faith of those aligned with the movement. First, they believe that the Bible is the supreme authority for faith and practice. Second, they believe in the essential of new birth, an experience of conversion through grace. Third, they believe in the centrality of the redeeming work of Christ. Fourth, they believe in the pressing need to evangelize the world. Fifth, they believe that the church is a community of believers indwelt by the Holy Spirit. These convictions to one degree or another have their roots in the classical Protestant doctrines of the Reformation (salvation-church-Bible). Thus the seedbed of what was to come was the Protestant Reformation.

After the Reformation, evangelicalism encountered its next formative phase in the revivals. Because Protestantism had become somewhat cold, lifeless and rational in its focus on dogma and formality, and because of the Enlightenment, evangelicalism highlighted the conversion experience, being "born again," having a heartfelt faith.

The third formative period of American evangelicalism was fundamentalism (1920–1960). Before 1920 it would not have been difficult to conceive of an evangelical dominance in American society. But this was no longer the case after the second decade of the twentieth century. The influx of immigrants had brought to America a plurality of religious beliefs and subcultures. The rise of the theory of evolution had made it popular to question the existence of a personal God as the sole originator of life. The idea of a miraculous new birth wrought by God seemed fictitious in this age of science. And to top it off, modernists were declaring that the Bible is untrustworthy, for they said it is merely an ancient document reflective of an ancient people's religious beliefs. Since it isn't permanently valid, it has to be read and dissected critically.

A symbol of the conflict in America was the Scopes trial of 1925. John T. Scopes was accused of breaking Tennessee law by teaching evolution. Clarence Darrow, a religious skeptic, headed his defense, and the fundamentalists placed their hopes for the prosecution in William Jennings Bryan. Darrow placed Bryan on the stand and proceeded to argue the apparent intellectual poverty of fundamentalism. Although Scopes was found guilty (a verdict later overturned by a higher court on a technicality), fundamentalism had received ridicule. To many in America, both modernist and fundamentalist, it appeared that the fundamentalists had lost the day—and their once respected place in the culture. They were now on the defensive.

As a result of the perceived advance of modernity, evangelicals (fundamentalists) entered into combat with modernists. The modernists attempted to reinterpret classical orthodoxy in a manner inoffensive to modern minds, often rejecting elements of that orthodoxy completely. The fundamentalists tried to reclaim American society. Two things happened. First, some fundamentalists gave up and gave in, and several mainline denominations became modern. Second, staunch fundamentalists separated from mainline denominations and formed independent churches and parachurch ministries, thereby forming a fundamentalist subculture outside the larger modernist culture. Fundamentalists surrendered the universities to the modernists and formed their own institutions of education.

Two negative results occurred because of this retreat from the larger society. First, Christians had the tendency to become focused on their own groups to the neglect of being "salt of the earth" or "the light of the world" (Mt 5:13-16). Second, some Christians came to view the mind, academics and intellectual excellence as less than godly. Associating the life of the mind with what led to modern liberalism, they chose emotionalism or experience over careful, precise thinking. They forgot that

Jesus had commanded us to "love the Lord your God with all
. . . your mind" (Mt 22:37).

Following World War II, some conservatives brought evangelicalism into its current phase. Conservatives like Carl F. H.
Henry (1913–) challenged Christians toward academic excellence and sensitivity toward the needs of a hurting society.
They challenged Christians to enter into dialogue with the
modern culture from a conservative viewpoint and to minister
to its needs mercifully, without being silent about or modifying
conversion or classical orthodoxy. From within Britain, too,
evangelicals such as the New Testament scholar F. F. Bruce
(1910–1991), the pastor John R. W. Stott (1921–) and the theologian J. I. Packer (1926–) contributed to the betterment of
evangelicalism. In America evangelicals organized to develop
the new vision. Already in 1942 Harold J. Ockenga (1905–1985)
and others had founded the National Association of Evangelicals (NAE). Ockenga later (1956) participated in L. Nelson
Bell's (1894–1973) and Billy Graham's (1918–) creation of the
evangelical periodical *Christianity Today.* Carl F. H. Henry
served as the first editor from 1956 to 1968. Evangelicals also
established new seminaries (for example, Fuller in 1947) and
the Evangelical Theological Society (1949).

One minister-evangelist has excelled in the vision. Though
he began his evangelistic ministry in 1944, it was a campaign in
Los Angeles in 1949 that thrust him into the national spotlight.
He founded his own evangelistic association and radio ministry in 1950 and furthered his ministry by writing. He is known
not only for his giftedness in evangelism but also for his service
to the executive branch of the United States government, for
his participation in international evangelistic conferences, for
his willingness to work with a diversity of traditions and for his
enduring integrity. His name? Of course, it's Billy Graham.

It is impossible, really, to finish the story. Franklin Graham
now serves in his father's stead. Evangelicalism goes on. Chris-

tian history goes on. Even as you read these lines the tale of the church, the bride of Christ, is unfolding. I find the sequence from the apostolic fathers to Billy Graham fascinating. I find the developments in just the last three hundred years remarkable. And my perspective for Christian life in the twenty-first century has been framed by all of it. Believing rightly, living in unity, praying devotedly, sacrificing selflessly, knowing God deeply, evangelizing globally, distinguishing culture from conversion and passing fads from eternal truths—it is to these ends that the past calls us.

But Christians are not merely to look back. The story goes on, and to remembrance the Bible teaches us to join the virtue of hope. Ultimately Christians are both a backward-looking and a forward-looking people, a people with historical discretion and confident expectation. Together, from every corner of the earth, throughout each century, they have gazed into what has been and have awaited the Son of Man who comes in the clouds. And so we say, Come, Lord Jesus.

Notes

Preface

¹Bill Cosby, *Kids Say the Darndest Things* (New York: Bantam, 1998), pp. 117–18.

²*The Wit and Wisdom of Will Rogers,* ed. Alex Ayers (London: Penguin, 1993), p. 105.

³Cosby, *Kids Say the Darndest Things,* p. 121.

⁴John of Salisbury, "The Metalogicon" 3.4, in *The Metalogicon of John Salisbury,* trans. Daniel D. McGarry (Gloucester, Mass.: Peter Smith, 1971), pp. 167–68 (italics added).

Part One: Diamonds

¹The artworks mentioned in this chapter are reproduced and discussed in Antonio Baruffa, *The Catacombs of St. Callixtus* (Vatican City: L. E. V., 1992), pp. 37, 111–12.

²Ibid., p. 137.

Chapter One: On the Heels of the Apostles

¹*The Apostolic Fathers: Greek Texts and English Translations of Their Writings,* 2nd ed., trans. and ed. J. B. Lightfoot and J. R. Harmer, rev. Michael W. Holmes (Grand Rapids, Mich.: Baker, 1992), p. 43.

²Ibid., p. 93.

³Ibid., p. 141.

⁴Ibid., pp. 185–87.

⁵Ibid., pp. 155–57.

[6]Ibid., p. 153.

[7]Ibid., p. 195

[8]Ibid., p. 145.

[9]Ibid., p. 181.

[10]Ibid., p. 155.

[11]Ibid., p. 171.

[12]"Martyrdom of Polycarp" 9.3, in *Apostolic Fathers,* p. 235.

[13]Ibid., 11.1–14.3, p. 235.

[14]"The Martyrdom of Saints Perpetua and Felicitas," in *The Acts of the Christian Martyrs,* ed. and trans. H. Musurillo (Oxford: Clarendon, 1972), pp. 106–31.

[15]"The Martyrdom of Martha, Daughter of Posi Who Was a Daughter of the Covenant," in *Holy Women of the Syrian Orient,* updated ed., trans. and intro. S. P. Brock and S. Ashbrook Harvey (Berkeley: University of California Press, 1987), pp. 67–73.

[16]The following discussion on Roman religion and its view of Christianity is based on R. L. Wilken, *The Christians as the Romans Saw Them* (New Haven, Conn.: Yale University Press, 1984), pp. 48–125. See also Wilken's article "Toward a Social Interpretation of Early Christian Apologetics," *Church History* 39 (1970): 437–58.

[17]Tertullian, "Apology" 35–36, trans. S. Thelwall, in *Latin Christianity: Its Founder, Tertullian,* The Ante-Nicene Fathers 3, ed. A. Roberts and J. Donaldson, rev. ed. A. C. Coxe (Grand Rapids, Mich.: Eerdmans, 1978), pp. 43–44.

[18]Celsus, quoted in Origen, *Against Celsus* 1.9; 6.110. See S. Benko, "Pagan Criticism of Christianity During the First Two Centuries A.D.," in *Aufstieg und Niedergang der Römischen Welt,* ed. H. Temporini and W. Hasse (Berlin: de Gruyter, 1980), p. 1100.

[19]Miniucius Felix, "Octavius" 8–9, trans. R. E. Wallis, in *Fathers of the Third Century,* Ante-Nicene Fathers 4, p. 177.

[20]Athenagoras, "A Plea Regarding Christians" 3, trans. C. C. Richardson, in *Early Christian Fathers,* Library of Christian Classics, ed. C. C. Richardson (Philadelphia: Westminster Press, 1953), p. 303.

[21]See Wilken's discussion of libertine Christian groups in *Christians as the Romans Saw Them,* pp. 19–21.

[22]R. T. France, *Matthew: Evangelist and Teacher* (Grand Rapids, Mich.: Zondervan, 1989), p. 269.

[23]"Diognetus" 6, trans. E. R. Fairweather, in Richardson, *Early Christian Fathers,* p. 218.

[24]"The First Apology of Justin the Martyr" 14, trans. E. R. Hardy, in Richardson, *Early Christian Fathers,* pp. 249–50.

[25]Athenagoras, "Plea Regarding Christians" 11–12, p. 310.

[26]Ibid., 34, p. 338.

[27]Francis Schaeffer, *The Mark of the Christian* (Downers Grove, Ill.: Inter-Varsity Press, 1975), pp. 14–15.

[28]Justin, "First Apology" 17, p. 253.

[29]Athenagoras, "Plea Regarding Christians," pp. 4–9.

[30]Irenaeus, "Against Heresies" 3.16.8, trans. A. Roberts and W. H. Rambaut, in *The Apostolic Fathers with Justin Martyr and Irenaeus,* Ante-Nicene Fathers 1, p. 443.

[31]Ibid., 3.17.4.

[32]M. E. Marty, *A Short History of Christianity,* 2nd ed. (Philadelphia: Fortress, 1987), p. 57.

Chapter Two: Councils of Doctrine, Cloisters of Holiness

[1]"Arius's Letter to Eusebius of Nicomedia," in *The Trinitarian Controversy,* ed. and trans. William G. Rusch (Philadelphia: Fortress, 1980), pp. 29–30.

[2]"The Creed of the Synod of Nicaea (June 19, 325)," quoted in Rusch, *Trinitarian Controversy,* p. 49.

[3]"The Constantinopolitan Creed (Creed of 150 Fathers)," in *Creeds of the Churches,* ed. J. H. Leith, 3rd ed. (Louisville, Ky.: John Knox Press, 1982), p. 33.

[4]Basil of Caesarea, "Epistle" 236.6, in *Creeds, Councils and Controversies,* ed. J. Stevenson, rev. ed. W. H. C. Frend (London: SPCK, 1989), p. 105.

[5]A. W. Tozer, *The Knowledge of the Holy* (New York: Harper & Row, 1961), pp. 9–12.

[6]"The Council of Chalcedon's 'Definition of the Faith,'" in *The Christological Controversy,* ed. and trans. R. A. Norris Jr. (Philadelphia: Fortress, 1980), p. 159.

[7]Marty, *Short History,* p. 47.

[8]Ibid., p. 48.

[9]D. Burton-Christie, *The Word in the Desert* (Oxford: Oxford University Press, 1993), p. 4.

[10]D. Burton-Christie, "Oral Culture, Biblical Interpretation, and Spirituality in Early Christian Monasticism," in *The Bible in Greek Christian Antiquity,* ed. and trans. P. M. Blowers (Notre Dame, Ind.: University of Notre Dame, 1997), p. 429 (italics his).

[11]In S. Baring-Gould, *The Lives of the Saints (August),* 2nd ed. (London: John Hodges, 1875), p. 340.

[12]"The Sayings of the Fathers, Part XVII, Of Charity 22," in *Western Asceticism,* Library of Christian Classics, ed. O. Chadwick (Philadelphia: Westminster Press, 1958), p. 186.

[13]"The Sayings of the Fathers, Part XV, Of Humility 54," in *Western Asceticism,* p. 168.

[14]Ibid., p. 167.

[15]Baring-Gould, *Lives of the Saints,* p. 341.

[16]Ibid., p. 342.

[17]Ibid., pp. 342–43.

[18]"Rule of Saint Benedict" 20, in *Western Asceticism,* p. 309.

Part Two: Emeralds

[1]These artworks are depicted in Edward G. Tasker, *Encyclopedia of Medieval Art* (London: Batsford, 1993), pp. 183–87.

Chapter Three: Empires, Emperors & Pastors

[1]Clovis, quoted in S. Baring-Gould, *The Lives of the Saints (October)* (London: John Hodges, 1877), p. 6.

[2]See J. van Engen, "Faith as a Concept of Order in Medieval Christendom," in *Belief in History,* ed. T. Kselman (Notre Dame, Ind.: University of Notre Dame, 1991), pp. 19–67.

[3]John Calvin, *Institutes of the Christian Religion* 3.2.7.

[4]Beryl Smalley, *The Study of the Bible in the Middle Ages* (Notre Dame, Ind.: University of Notre Dame Press, 1978), p. xi.

[5]B. Ward, "Mysticism and Devotion on the Middle Ages," in *Companion Encyclopedia of Theology,* ed. P. Byrne and L. Houlden (London: Routledge, 1995), p. 558.

[6]Aelred of Rievaulx, "The Consolations of Scripture," in *The Cistercian World,* trans. and ed. P. Matarasso (London: Penguin, 1993), p. 193.

[7]Gregory the Great, *Morals on the Book of Job,* pref. 4, quoted in B. McGinn, *The Growth of Mysticism* (New York: Crossroad Herder, 1996), p. 40.

[8]Ibid., p. 39.

[9]See A. C. Rush, "Spiritual Martyrdom in St. Gregory the Great," *Theological Studies* 23 (1962): 569–89.

[10]"Homilies on the Gospels" 1, in *Gregory the Great, Forty Gospel Homilies,* Cistercian Studies, no. 123, trans. D. Hurst (Kalamazoo, Mich.: Cistercian, 1990), pp. 8–9.

[11]"Homilies on the Gospels" 27, in *Forty Gospel Homilies,* p. 214 (italics his).

[12]Ibid., 35, p. 307.

[13]See G. R. Evans, *The Thought of Gregory the Great* (Cambridge: Cambridge University Press, 1986), pp. 80–85.

[14]"Homilies on Ezekiel" 1.10.13, quoted in Evans, *Thought of Gregory the Great,* p. 85.

[15]"Homilies on the Gospels" 30, in *Forty Gospel Homilies,* pp. 238–39.

[16]See *Morals on the Book of Job* 21.15.22; 5.22.44; 18.43.70; 14.51.59; 13.4.4; 1.5.6. See also Evans, *Thought of Gregory the Great,* pp. 72–74.

[17]Selections from "Gregory, The Book of Pastoral Rule" 2.2–11, trans. J. Barnby, slightly altered, in *Leo the Great and Gregory the Great,* Nicene and Post-Nicene Fathers, 2nd series, no. 12, ed. Philip Schaff and H. Wace (Grand Rapids, Mich.: Eerdmans, 1979), pp. 9–23.

[18]*"De duodecim abusivis saeculi,"* in M. L. W. Laistner, *Thought and Letters in Western Europe: A.D. 500 to 900* (Ithaca, N.Y.: Cornell University Press, 1966), p. 144.

[19]V. Green, *A New History of Christianity* (New York: Continuum, 1996), p. 58.

[20]R. W. Southern, *The Making of the Middle Ages* (New Haven, Conn.: Yale University Press, 1953), p. 161.

Chapter Four: Medieval Lessons on Prayer, Thinking & Devotion

[1]This material first appeared as "The Practice of Prayer in Early and Medieval Monasticism" in *Bibliotheca Sacra* 158 (January–March 2001): 104–15. It is used here by permission. See also G. Tellenbach, *The Church in Western Europe from the Tenth to the Early Twelfth Century* (Cambridge: Cambridge University Press, 1993), pp. 101–7; J. Leclercq, "Ways of Prayer and Contemplation: II. Western," in *Christian Spirituality: Origins to the Twelfth Century,* ed. B. McGinn, J. Meyendorff and J. Leclercq (New York: Crossroad, 1996), pp. 415–26; and B. Ward,

"Mysticism and Devotion in the Middle Ages," in *Companion Encyclopedia of Theology,* ed. P. Byrne and L. Houlden (London and New York: Routledge, 1995), pp. 558–75. For introductions on monasticism, see D. Knowles, *Christian Monasticism* (New York: McGraw-Hill, 1969); C. H. Lawrence, *Medieval Monasticism: Forms of Religious Life in Western Europe in the Middle Ages,* 2nd ed. (London and New York: Longman, 1989); L. J. Daly, *Benedictine Monasticism: Its Formation and Development Through the Twelfth Century* (New York: Sheed & Ward, 1965); J. E. Goehring, "Monasticism," in *Encyclopedia of Early Christianity,* 2nd ed., ed. E. Ferguson (New York: Garland, 1997), pp. 769–74.

[2]Athanasius of Alexandria, "Life of Antony" 3, in *Early Christian Lives,* ed. and trans. C. White (London: Penguin, 1998), 10.3.

[3]Bernard of Clairvaux, "Sermon on Advent" 9, quoted in Leclercq, "Ways of Prayer and Contemplation," p. 423.

[4]*"Monumenta Germaniae Historica, Diplomata, Henry III,"* no. 263, quoted in Tellenbach, *Church in Western Europe,* p. 107.

[5]In S. Baring-Gould, *The Lives of the Saints (June),* 2nd ed. (London: John Hodges, 1874), p. 120.

[6]"The Old English Benedictine Office," in *Anglo-Saxon Poetry,* trans. and ed. S. A. J. Bradley (London: Everyman's Library, 1997), p. 539.

[7]"The Rule of Saint Benedict" 20, in *Western Asceticism,* Library of Christian Classics, ed. O. Chadwick (Philadelphia: Westminster Press, 1958), pp. 309–10.

[8]G. S. M. Walker, ed., *S. Columbani Opera* (Dublin: Institute for Advanced Studies, 1957), cited in J. Leclercq, "Liturgy and Contemplation," trans. S. P. Manning, *Monastic Studies* 10 (1974): 82. Cf. idem, "Meditation as Biblical Reading," *Worship* 33 (1959): 564.

[9]*"Expositio in Regulam S. Benedicti"* 20, cited in Leclercq, "Liturgy and Contemplation," p. 82. Cf. idem, "Meditation as Biblical Reading," p. 565.

[10]Cassian, "Conferences" 9.24, in *Western Asceticism,* p. 226.

[11]Aelred of Rievaulx, "Pastoral Prayer," in *The Cistercian World: Monastic Writings of the Twelfth Century,* ed. and trans. P. Matarasso (London: Penguin, 1993), pp. 194–98.

[12]Anselm, "Prayer for Enemies" 16–18, 37–39, 46–52, in *Prayers and Meditations of Saint Anselm with the Proslogion,* trans. B. Ward (London:

Penguin, 1973), pp. 216–17.

[13]Cassian, "Conferences" 9.3, p. 215.

[14]Ibid., 10.14, p. 245.

[15]D. Burton-Christie, *The Word in the Desert: Scripture and the Quest for Holiness in Early Christian Monasticism* (Oxford: Oxford University Press, 1993), pp. 163–64, relating Lucious 1.

[16]*"Speculum Monachorum"* 1, quoted in J. Leclercq, *The Love of Learning and the Desire for God: A Study of Monastic Culture,* trans. C. Misrahi (New York: Fordham University Press, 1982), p. 73.

[17]Anselm, "Meditation on Human Redemption" 4–12, in *Prayers and Meditations,* p. 230.

[18]Ward, introduction to *Prayers and Meditations,* pp. 43–44.

[19]Antony of Padua, quoted in Baring-Gould, *Lives of the Saints (June),* p. 184.

[20]"Sayings of the Fathers," Epiphanius 3, quoted in *The Desert Christian: Sayings of the Desert Fathers,* trans. B. Ward (New York: Macmillan, 1975), p. 57.

[21]See J. Dyer, "The Psalms in Monastic Prayer," in *The Place of the Psalms in the Intellectual Culture of the Middle Ages,* ed. N. van Deusen (Albany: State University of New York Press, 1999), pp. 9–89.

[22]"Sayings of the Fathers," Epiphanius 11 and Antony 3, p. 58.

[23]Leclercq, "Liturgy and Contemplation," pp. 80–84.

[24]"Rules of Pachomius" 2.166, quoted in W. A. Graham, *Beyond the Written Word* (Cambridge: Cambridge University Press, 1987), p. 130.

[25]"Rules of Pachomius" 3.210.

[26]Leclercq, "Liturgy and Contemplation," p. 86.

[27]Anselm, "Prayer to Christ" 158-81, in *Prayers and Meditations,* p. 98.

[28]Anselm, *"Proslogion"* 1.1-7, 35-46, 50-51, 65-66, 86-88, 126-29; 9.332-35; 14.456-58, in *Prayers and Meditations,* pp. 239–43, 250, 255.

[29]Anselm, "Meditation on Human Redemption" 25–33, 163–67, pp 230–31, 234.

[30]Cassian, "Conferences" 10.10, p. 240.

[31]Ibid., pp. 240–43.

[32]Eadmer, *The Life of Saint Anselm, Archbishop of Canterbury,* ed. and trans. R. W. Southern (Oxford: Oxford University Press, 1962), p. 14.

[33]T. Gilby, "Appendix 2. Method of the Summa," in *St. Thomas Aquinas Summa Theologiae* (New York: McGraw-Hill, 1964), p. 48.

[34]*Summa Theologiae* 1a.1–8, trans. T. Gilby, in *Summa Theologiae,* pp. 29–31.

[35]Anselm, *"Proslogion"* 1.155–57, p. 244.

[36]See W. Jay Wood, *Epistemology: Becoming Intellectually Virtuous* (Downers Grove, Ill.: InterVarsity Press, 1998), pp. 18–31.

[37]See E. Underhill, "Medieval Mysticism," in *The Cambridge Medieval History,* Decline of Empire and Papacy 7, ed. J. R. Tanner et al. (Cambridge: Cambridge University Press, 1949), pp. 777–812; R. N. Swanson, *Religion and Devotion in Europe, c. 1215–c. 1515,* Cambridge Medieval Textbooks (Cambridge: Cambridge University Press, 1995), pp. 172–82; Ward, "Mysticism and Devotion in the Middle Ages"; and C. Butler, *Western Mysticism* (New York: Dutton, 1924).

[38]See the discussion in Cuthbert, *Western Mysticism,* pp. 279–326, on the biblical thinking of the medieval mystics.

[39]Bernard of Clairvaux, "On the Love of God" 1.7, in *Late Medieval Mysticism,* Library of Christian Classics, ed. R. C. Petry (Philadelphia: Westminster Press, 1957), pp. 54–55 (italics his).

[40]Meister Eckhart, "On Solitude and the Attainment of God," in *Late Medieval Mysticism,* p. 201.

[41]C. Walker Bynum, *Jesus as Mother: Studies in the Spirituality of the High Middle Ages* (Berkeley: University of California Press, 1982), pp. 261, 184–85.

[42]Ibid., p. 262.

[43]Ibid., pp. 129–30, 261.

[44]Julian of Norwich, "Book of Showings" 59, in *A Lesson of Love: The Revelations of Julian of Norwich,* ed. and trans. J. Julian (New York: Walker, 1988), pp. 154–55.

[45]Ibid., 5, pp. 12–13.

[46]E. H. Peterson, *Subversive Spirituality* (Grand Rapids, Mich.: Eerdmans, 1997), pp. 35–36.

Chapter Five: A River with Many Tributaries

[1]See R. Williams, "Religious Experience in the Era of Reform," in *Companion Encyclopedia of Theology,* ed. P. Bryne and L. Houlden (London: Routledge, 1995), pp. 576–80.

[2]Erasmus, *The Handbook of the Christian Soldier,* fifth rule, in *The Erasmus Reader,* ed. E. Rummel (Toronto: University of Toronto Press,

1990), p. 152.

[3]Ibid., p. 151.

[4]Erasmus, *Apology Against the Dialogue of Latomus,* 40.

[5]See M. O'Boyle, *Erasmus on Language and Method in Theology* (Toronto: University of Toronto Press, 1977), p. 130.

[6]Erasmus, *Apology Against Latomus,* 5, 30.

[7]G. R. Potter, *Zwingli* (Cambridge: Cambridge University Press, 1976), pp. 39–40.

[8]See Steven E. Ozment, *The Age of Reform: 1250–1550* (New Haven, Conn.: Yale University Press, 1980), pp. 302–9.

[9]Erasmus, *The Free Will* 7, in *Erasmus–Luther: Discourse on Free Will,* trans. and ed. E. F. Winter (New York: Continuum, 1996), pp. 11–12.

[10]Ozment, *Age of Reform,* p. 309.

[11]See M. L. Colish, *Medieval Foundations of the Western Intellectual Tradition 400–1400* (New Haven, Conn.: Yale University Press, 1997), pp. 253–62.

[12]Ozment, *Age of Reform,* pp. 233–39.

[13]Martin Luther, *Disputation Against Scholastic Theology* 7, 30, 34, in *Martin Luther's Basic Theological Writings,* ed. T. F. Lull (Minneapolis: Fortress Press, 1989), pp. 13, 15.

Chapter Six: The Doctrine of Salvation in the Reformers

[1]Martin Luther, "Disputation" 4, 40, in *Martin Luther's Basic Theological Writings,* ed. T. F. Lull (Minneapolis: Fortress, 1989), pp. 13, 16.

[2]Martin Luther, "The Ninety-Five Theses," in *Basic Theological Writings,* pp. 24–26.

[3]See B. Drewery, "Martin Luther," in *A History of Christian Doctrine,* ed. H. Cunliffe-Jones with B. Drewery (Philadelphia: Fortress, 1981), p. 317.

[4]Martin Luther, "Letter 21 to John von Staupitz," in *Letters 1,* Luther's Works 48, ed. and trans. G. G. Krodel (Philadelphia: Fortress, 1963), p. 65.

[5]Ibid., pp. 66–67.

[6]Quoted in H. Hillerbrand, ed., *The Reformation: A Narrative History Related by Contemporary Observers and Participants* (Grand Rapids, Mich.: Baker, 1994), p. 27.

[7]Martin Luther, "Two Kinds of Righteousness," in *Basic Theological*

Writings, p. 156.

[8]Ibid., p. 157.

[9]Martin Luther, "A Commentary on St. Paul's Epistle to the Galatians," in *Martin Luther: Selections from His Writings,* ed. John Dillenberger (New York: Doubleday, 1962), p. 130.

[10]Martin Luther, "Freedom of a Christian," in *Martin Luther: Selections from His Writings,* pp. 52–53.

[11]Ibid., p. 53.

[12]John Calvin, "Reply to Letter by Cardinal Sadolet to the Senate and People of Geneva," in *John Calvin: Selection from His Writings,* ed. John Dillenberger (Garden City, N.Y.: Doubleday, 1971), p. 110.

[13]Quoted in Dillenberger, *John Calvin: Selections from His Writings,* pp. 424–25.

[14]Quoted in Dillenberger, *John Calvin: Selections from His Writings,* p. 470.

[15]Ibid., p. 471.

Chapter Seven: The Doctrines of the Church & the Scriptures in the Reformers

[1]Martin Luther, "On the Councils and the Church," in *Martin Luther's Basic Theological Writings*, ed. T. F. Lull (Minneapolis: Fortress, 1989), pp. 545-50.

[2]Ibid., pp. 551-61.

[3]Martin Luther, "Preface to the Wittenberg Edition of Luther's German Writings," in *Basic Theological Writings,* p. 64.

[4]Martin Luther, "What to Look for and Expect in the Gospels," in *Basic Theological Writings,* pp. 104–11.

[5]Ibid., p. 109.

[6]Cf. Romans 1:1-4; 1 Peter 1:10-11; Acts 3:24; Luke 24:44-47.

[7]John Calvin, *Commentary on Exodus,* 20.8.

Chapter Eight: The Enlightenment & Modernity

[1]Horace, "Epistles" 2.40, quoted in J. Pelikan, *Christian Doctrine and Modern Culture (Since 1700),* The Christian Tradition 5 (Chicago: University of Chicago Press, 1989), p. 60.

[2]Immanuel Kant, "Answer to the Question: What Is Enlightenment?" quoted in Pelikan, *Christian Doctrine and Modern Culture (Since 1700),* p. 60.

[3]Alexander Pope, quoted in N. Hampson, *The Enlightenment,* The Pelican History of European Thought 4 (Baltimore: Penguin, 1968), p. 38.

[4]Paul Holbach, *System of Nature,* quoted in *A Dictionary of Philosophy,* 2nd ed., s.v. "Enlightenment."

[5]Paul Holbach, quoted in E. Cassirer, *The Philosophy of the Enlightenment* (Princeton, N.J.: Princeton University Press, 1951), p. 70.

[6]Anselm, *"Proslogion"* 1.150–57, in *The Prayers and Meditations of Saint Anselm with the Proslogion,* ed. B. Ward (London: Penguin, 1973), p. 244.

[7]A. Dulles, *The Assurance of Things Hoped For* (New York: Oxford University Press, 1994), pp. 274–75.

[8]A. E. McGrath, ed., *The Blackwell Encyclopedia of Modern Christian Thought,* s.v. "Enlightenment."

Chapter Nine: Awakenings & Revivals

[1]Jonathan Edwards, "A Divine and Supernatural Light," in *A Jonathan Edwards Reader,* ed. J. E. Smith, H. S. Stout and K. P. Minkema (New Haven, Conn.: Yale University Press, 1995), pp. 105–24.

[2]Jonathan Edwards, "The Distinguishing Marks," in *Jonathan Edwards: The Great Awakening,* The Works of Jonathan Edwards 4, ed. C. C. Goen (New Haven, Conn.: Yale University Press, 1972), pp. 214–88.

[3]Ibid., pp. 255–56.

[4]Jonathan Edwards, "A Treatise Concerning Religious Affections," in *Jonathan Edwards Reader,* p. 141.

[5]Ibid., p. 148.

[6]Ibid., p. 165. Edwards cited four passages from the Bible in support: 2 Corinthians 5:15, Ephesians 2:10, Titus 2:14, and Hebrews 9:14.

[7]Charles G. Finney, *Lectures on Revivals of Religion,* rev. ed. (Oberlin, Ohio: E. J. Goodrich, 1868), p. 12.

[8]Ibid.

[9]In Charles G. Finney, *Sermons on Important Subjects* (New York: John S. Taylor, 1836), pp. 3–43.

[10]In Charles G. Finney, *Sermons on Gospel Themes* (New York: Revell, 1876), p. 207.

[11]Ibid., p. 208.

[12]Ibid., p. 212.

[13]M. A. Noll, *The Scandal of the Evangelical Mind* (Grand Rapids, Mich.: Eerdmans, 1994), p. 64.

[14]See G. Wacker, "America's Pentecostals: Who They Are," *Christianity Today,* October 16, 1987, pp. 16–21.

Chapter 10: Liberalism, Missions & Evangelicalism

[1]Henry Ward Beecher, quoted in W. S. Hudson, *Religion in America,* 3rd ed. (New York: Charles Scribner's Sons, 1981), pp. 268–69.

[2]Shailer Matthews, *Faith of Modernism* (New York: Macmillan, 1924), p. 22.

[3]Statistics for much of this discussion may be found in D. B. Barrett and T. M. Johnson, "Annual Statistical Table on Global Mission: 2001," *International Bulletin of Missionary Research* 25 (2001): 24–25.

[4]*Evangelical Dictionary of World Missions,* s.v. "Bible Translation."

[5]"The Status of Christianity and Religions in the Modern World," in *World Christianity Encyclopedia,* 2nd ed., 2 vols., ed. D. B. Barrett, G. T. Kurian and T. M. Johnson (New York: Oxford University Press, 2001), 1:3.

[6]*Evangelical Dictionary of World Missions,* s.v. "Non-Western Mission Boards and Societies."

Bibliography

General Church History

Ackroyd, P. R., et al. *The Cambridge History of the Bible.* 3 vols. Cambridge: Cambridge University Press, 1970.

Barrett, David B., ed. *World Christian Encyclopedia.* New York: Oxford University Press, 1982.

Bettenson, Henry, ed. *Documents of the Christian Church.* 2nd ed. New York: Oxford University Press, 1963.

Brauer, Jerald C., ed. *The Westminster Dictionary of Church History.* Philadelphia: Westminster Press, 1971.

Cairns, Earl E. *Christianity Through the Centuries.* Rev. ed. Grand Rapids, Mich.: Zondervan, 1981.

Chadwick, Henry, and G. R. Evans, eds. *Atlas of the Christian Church.* New York: Facts on File, 1987.

Clouse, Robert G., et al. *Two Kingdoms: The Church and Culture Through the Ages.* Chicago: Moody Press, 1993.

Cross, F. L., and E. A. Livingstone, eds. *The Oxford Dictionary of the Christian Church.* 3rd ed. New York: Oxford University Press, 1997.

Douglas, J. D., ed. *The New International Dictionary of the Christian Church.* Grand Rapids, Mich.: Zondervan, 1974.

Dowley, Tim, ed. *Introduction to the History of Christianity.* Minneapolis: Fortress, 1995.

Kelly, J. N. D. *The Oxford Dictionary of the Popes.* Oxford: Oxford University Press, 1986.

Latourette, Kenneth Scott. *Christianity Through the Ages.* New York: HarperCollins, 1965.

———. *A History of Christianity.* Rev. ed. 2 vols. New York: HarperCollins, 1975.

Leith, J. H., ed. *Creeds of the Churches.* 3rd ed. Louisville, Ky.: John Knox Press, 1982.

Marty, Martin E. *A Short History of Christianity.* 2nd ed. Philadelphia: Fortress, 1987.

McManners, John, ed. *The Oxford Illustrated History of Christianity.* Oxford: Oxford University Press, 1990.

Neill, Stephen. *A History of Christian Missions.* Rev. ed. London: Penguin, 1986.

Noll, Mark A. *Turning Points.* Grand Rapids, Mich.: Baker, 1997.

Placher, William C., ed. *Readings in the History of Christian Theology.* 2 vols. Philadelphia: Westminster Press, 1988.

Schaff, Philip. *The Creeds of Christendom.* 6th ed. 3 vols. New York: Harper, 1919. Reprint, Grand Rapids, Mich.: Baker, 1985.

————. *History of the Christian Church.* 8 vols. New York: Charles Scribner's Sons, 1910. Reprint, Grand Rapids, Mich.: Eerdmans, 1960.

Shelley, Bruce. *Church History in Plain Language.* Waco, Tex.: Word, 1982.

Vos, Howard F. *Exploring Church History.* Nashville: Thomas Nelson, 1994.

Walker, Williston, et al. *A History of the Christian Church.* 4th ed. New York: Charles Scribner's Sons, 1985.

Walton, Robert. *Chronological and Background Charts of Church History.* Grand Rapids, Mich.: Zondervan, 1986.

White, James F. *A Brief History of Christian Worship.* Nashville: Abingdon, 1993.

The Early Church

Berardino, Angelo Di, ed. *Encyclopedia of the Early Church.* 2 vols. New York: Oxford University Press, 1992.

Chadwick, Henry. *The Early Church.* London: Penguin, 1967.

Daniélou, Jean, and Henri Marrou. *The First Six Hundred Years.* The Christian Centuries 1. Translated by V. Cronin. London: Darton, Longman & Todd, 1983.

Ferguson, Everett, ed. *Encyclopedia of Early Christianity.* 2nd ed. 2 vols. New York: Garland, 1997.

Frend, W. H. C. *The Rise of Christianity.* Philadelphia: Fortress, 1984.

The Church in the Middle Ages

Knowles, David, and Dimitri Obolensky. *The Middle Ages.* The Christian Centuries 2. London: Darton, Longman & Todd, 1979.

Southern, R. W. *The Making of the Middle Ages.* New Haven, Conn.: Yale University Press, 1953.

————. *Western Society and the Church in the Middle Ages.* London: Penguin, 1970.

Strayer, J. R., ed. *Dictionary of the Middle Ages.* 13 vols. New York: Charles Scribner's Sons, 1982.

The Church in the Protestant Reformation

Cameron, Euan. *The European Reformation*. Oxford: Clarendon, 1991.

Chadwick, Owen. *The Reformation*. London: Penguin, 1972.

George, Timothy. *Theology of the Reformers*. Nashville: Broadman, 1988.

Hillerbrand, H. J., ed. *The Oxford Encyclopedia of the Reformation*. 4 vols. Oxford: Oxford University Press, 1996.

Lindberg, Carter. *The European Reformations*. Oxford: Blackwell, 1996.

McGrath, Alister. *The Intellectual Origins of the European Reformation*. Grand Rapids, Mich.: Baker, 1987.

————. *Reformation Thought*. 2nd ed. Oxford: Blackwell, 1993.

Oberman, Heiko A. *The Impact of the Reformation*. Grand Rapids, Mich.: Eerdmans, 1994.

————. *The Reformation: Roots and Ramifications*. Grand Rapids, Mich.: Eerdmans, 1994.

Ozment, Steven E. *The Age of Reform: 1250–1550*. New Haven, Conn.: Yale University Press, 1980.

————. *Protestants: The Birth of a Revolution*. Garden City, N.Y.: Doubleday, 1992.

Spitz, Lewis W. *The Protestant Reformation*. New York: Harper & Row, 1985.

The Church in the Modern Era

Ahlstrom, Sydney. *A Religious History of the American People*. New Haven, Conn.: Yale University Press, 1972.

Cairns, Earle E. *Christianity in the United States*. Chicago: Moody Press, 1964.

Gaustad, E. S., ed. *A Documentary History of Religion in America*. 2 vols. Grand Rapids, Mich.: Eerdmans, 1983.

————. *A Religious History of America*. New York: HarperCollins, 1966.

————. *Faith of Our Fathers*. New York: HarperCollins, 1987.

Hordern, William E. *A Layman's Guide to Protestant Orthodoxy*. Rev. ed. New York: Macmillan, 1955.

Hudson, Winthrop S. *Religion in America*. 3rd ed. New York: Charles Scribner's Sons, 1981.

Marty, Martin E. *Modern American Religion*. 3 vols. Chicago: University of Chicago Press, 1986.

McGrath, Alister. *The Blackwell Encyclopedia of Modern Christian Thought*. Oxford: Blackwell, 1993.

Mead, Frank S. *Handbook of Denominations in the United States*. 10th ed. Revised by Samuel S. Hill. Nashville: Abingdon, 1995.

Noll, Mark A. *A History of Christianity in the United States and Canada*. Grand Rapids, Mich.: Eerdmans, 1992.

Noll, Mark A., et al., eds. *Eerdmans Handbook to Christianity in America*. Grand Rapids, Mich.: Eerdmans, 1983.

Reid, Daniel G., et al., eds. *Dictionary of Christianity in America*. Downers

Grove, Ill.: InterVarsity Press, 1990.

Sweet, William W. *The Story of Religion in America.* Rev. ed. New York: Harper Collins, 1950. Reprint, Grand Rapids, Mich.: Baker, 1973.

Wuthnow, Robert. *Christianity in the Twenty-First Century.* Oxford: Oxford University Press, 1993.

Biographical Studies

Bainton, Roland H. *Here I Stand: A Life of Martin Luther.* New York: Abingdon, 1950.

Brown, Peter. *Augustine of Hippo: A Biography.* Berkeley and Los Angeles: University of California Press, 1969.

Cohn-Sherbok, Lavinia. *Who's Who in Christianity.* London: Routledge, 1998.

Dallimore, A. A. *George Whitefield.* 2 vols. Westchester, Ill.: Cornerstone, 1980.

Douglas, J. D., ed. *Twentieth-Century Dictionary of Christian Biography.* Grand Rapids, Mich.: Baker, 1995.

Douglas, J. D., and P. W. Comfort, eds. *Who's Who in Christian History.* Wheaton, Ill.: Tyndale House, 1992.

Miller, Perry. *Jonathan Edwards.* New York: Sloan Associates, 1949.

Parker, T. H. L. *John Calvin: A Biography.* Philadelphia: Westminster Press, 1975.

Potter, G. R. *Zwingli.* Cambridge: Cambridge University Press, 1976.

Wace, Henry, and W. C. Piercy, eds. *A Dictionary of Christian Biography.* Peabody, Mass.: Hendrickson, 1994.

Woodbridge, John D. *Great Leaders of the Christian Church.* Chicago: Moody Press, 1988.

Subject Index

Adam, 42, 48-49, 87
adoptionism, 40
Aelred of Rievaulx,
   67, 79-81, 170, 172
Africa, 63-64, 101,
   110, 155, 158-60
African American,
   148, 160
African Methodist
   Episcopal Church,
   160
Alexander of
   Alexandria, 46, 48
Alexandria, 46-47, 54,
   75, 172
Allen, Richard, 160
America, American,
   15, 137, 143, 147,
   153-64
American Baptist
   Missionary Union,
   155
American Board of
   Commissioners for
   Foreign Missions,
   155
Anabaptists, 124
Andover Seminary,
   155-56
Anglican, 155
Anselm, archbishop
   of Canterbury, 81-
   89, 92, 133-34, 172-
   73, 177
Antioch, 20, 22
Antony of Egypt, 55-
   56, 75, 84, 172

Antony of Padua, 84
apartheid, 160
Apollinarius of
   Laodicea, 51
apologists, 30-37
apostles, 19-21, 23,
   25-27, 41-43, 82, 90,
   115, 125, 134, 141
apostolic fathers, 19-
   31, 165
Aquinas, Thomas,
   92, 173
Arabs, 64
Arius, Arianism, 46-
   49, 64-65, 131, 169
Arminius,
   Arminianism, 144
Arnoul of Bohériss,
   83
Asbury, Francis, 160
asceticism, 55-56, 95,
   170, 172
Assemblies of God,
   148
Athanasius of
   Alexandria, 47-49,
   75, 172
Athenagoras of
   Athens, 32-36, 168-
   69
Athenagoras,
   patriarch of
   Constantinople, 91
atonement, doctrine
   of, 146, 149
Augustine of Hippo,
   110, 113, 119, 121,
   182
authority, 19, 25, 55,
   72, 89-92, 95, 97,
   109-10, 113, 118,
   125, 132-33, 143,
   150, 153, 162

Avignon, 109
awakenings, see
   Great Awakening,
   First, Second
baptism, 66, 122, 124
Baptist Missionary
   Society, 154
Baptists, 144, 154-55,
   160
Barth, Karl, 152
Basil of Caesarea, 50,
   55
Beecher, Henry
   Ward, 153
Belgium, 55, 63
Bell, L. Nelson, 164
Benedict of Nursia,
   Benedictine, 55-56,
   58-59, 73-74, 78-79,
   170, 172
Berkeley, George,
   130
Bernard of Chartres,
   13
Bernard of
   Clairvaux, 76, 96,
   172, 174
Bible, 12, 20, 38, 40,
   41-44, 46, 52, 55-57,
   67-68, 76, 83-86, 89,
   105, 107, 109, 124-
   26, 130-32, 135, 140,
   148, 150-54, 157-59,
   162, 165, 170, 177,
   178, 179
Biel, Gabriel, 111
bishops, 20-22, 25-26,
   41-42, 47, 72, 110,
   123
body, 16, 24, 27, 29,
   32-33, 39-41, 48, 53,
   85, 88, 95-96, 106,
   146